A scene from the New York Theatre Workshop production of "Quills." Set design by Neil Patel.

QUILLS

BY DOUG WRIGHT

★

★

DRAMATISTS
PLAY SERVICE
INC.

QUILLS
Copyright © 1996, Doug Wright

All Rights Reserved

SPECIAL NOTE

/one receiving permission to produce QUILLS is required (1) to give credit to
Author as sole and exclusive Author of the Play on the title page of all
grams distributed in connection with performances of the Play and in all
ances in which the title of the Play appears for purposes of advertising,
licizing or otherwise exploiting the Play and/or a production thereof. The
ie of the Author must appear on a separate line, in which no other name
ears, immediately beneath the title and in size of type equal to 50% of the
;est, most prominent letter used for the title of the Play. No person, firm or
ity may receive credit larger or more prominent than that accorded the Author;
l (2) to give the following acknowledgment on the title page of all programs
tributed in connection with performances of the Play:

:~inally produced in New York by the New York Theatre Workshop (1995)
Jim Nicola, Artistic Director
Nancy Kassak Diekmann, Managing

QUILLS was produced by New York Theatre Workshop (James C. Nicola, Artistic Director; Nancy Kassak Diekmann, Managing Director) in New York City, on November 3, 1995. It was directed by Howard Shalwitz; the set design was by Neil Patel; the costume design was by James Schuette; the lighting design was by Blake Burba; the sound design was by Darron L. West and the production stage manager was Kate Broderick. The cast was as follows:

DOCTOR ROYER-COLLARD .... Daniel Oreskes
MONSIEUR PROUIX; A LUNATIC .... Kirk Jackson
RENÉE PÉLAGIE .... Lola Pashalinski
ABBE de COULMIER .... Jefferson Mays
THE MARQUIS .... Rocco Sisto
MADELEINE LECLERC;
MADAME ROYER-COLLARD .... Katy Wales Selverstone

CHARACTERS

(In order of appearance)

DOCTOR ROYER-COLLARD — Chief physician of the Charenton asylum

MONSIEUR PROUIX — A celebrated architect

RENÉE PÉLAGIE — The grief-stricken wife of a madman

ABBE de COULMIER — Administrator at the asylum

THE MARQUIS — The asylum's most notorious inmate

MADELEINE LECLERC — The seamstress at Charenton; sixteen and quite lovely

A LUNATIC — A madman heard through a chink in the wall

MADAME ROYER-COLLARD — The Doctor's wife, a woman of considerable appetites

A NOTE ABOUT CASTING

The same actor may portray MONSIEUR PROUIX and the LUNATIC. Similarly, the same actress may double in the roles of MADELEINE and MADAME ROYER-COLLARD.

TIME

1807

PLACE

The Charenton Asylum; the office of Dr. ROYER-COLLARD, the quarters of the MARQUIS, and the hospital's charnel house.

A NOTE ON STYLE

The play is written, I hope, with all the fervor and self-consciousness of true melodrama.

Events in the play are not *cruel*; they are *diabolical*. Characters are not *good* or *bad*; they are either *kissed by God* or *yoked in Satan's merciless employ*.

Similarly, the play should be acted in a heightened, even archaic style. As grotesquerie mounts on grotesquerie, the play's passages should acquire an almost absurdist tone.

The sensational stagecraft of the *grand guignol* — thunder sheets, blood packets, rubber body parts and sleight of hand — all might find a home onstage. Before appealing to the audience's hearts or minds, the play endeavors to appeal to forces far more primal.

Fanaticism in me is the product of the persecutions I have endured from my tyrants. The longer they continue their vexations, the deeper they root my principles in my heart.

— The Marquis de Sade
in a Letter to His Wife

QUILLS

ACT ONE

Scene 1

Dr. Royer-Collard, Monsieur Prouix.

DR. ROYER-COLLARD.   I trust you are discreet, Monsieur Prouix. The delicacy of my situation here requires a candor far greater than I would otherwise employ.

MONSIEUR PROUIX.   Have no fear, Doctor. There's room in my grave for your secrets, as well as my own.

DR. ROYER-COLLARD.   I am the newly appointed Chief Physician of the Charenton Asylum. It is my solemn duty to restore this ailing institution to its former glory. I hope you won't accuse me of grandiosity if I suggest that Charenton is my France, and I am her Napoleon.

MONSIEUR PROUIX.   It's a metaphor both stirring and apt!

DR. ROYER-COLLARD.   The Ministry has granted me this post because — in their generous estimation — I am a staunchly moral man, of impeccable character and iron resolve. My wife, on the other hand, is less stalwart than I.

MONSIEUR PROUIX.   Oh, dear.

DR. ROYER-COLLARD.   She has a frivolous nature and boundless appetites which render her...

MONSIEUR PROUIX.   Yes?

DR. ROYER-COLLARD.   ... *prone to inconstancy.*

MONSIEUR PROUIX.   So many women are, Doctor! Their constitutions are not so fully evolved as our own. They fall prey to seduction as readily as you or I catch a summer cold.

DR. ROYER-COLLARD.   Often I've been tempted to chain

her at the heel, or secure a cow bell 'round her neck, so I'll be kept alert of her whereabouts.

MONSIEUR PROUIX.   Many a man has enforced worse measures in the name of Fidelity.

DR. ROYER-COLLARD.   While I was delighted to accept this post in the provinces, she was loathe to leave Paris. I forced her to abandon all she holds most dear. Her art teacher. Her gardener. And a frisky little footman named Hercule.

MONSIEUR PROUIX.   But she followed you here to Saint Maurice, nonetheless. Perhaps she favors her husband after all.

DR. ROYER-COLLARD.   It was bribery, not steadfastness, which enticed her. I promised her a chateau to rival Fontainebleau.

MONSIEUR PROUIX.   Hence, my employ ...

DR. ROYER-COLLARD.   You must construct a home of such grand design, so full of beauty and diversion, that she is never inclined to leave it.

MONSIEUR PROUIX.   I spent all morning, sir, in pursuit of that very end.

DR. ROYER-COLLARD.   And — ?

MONSIEUR PROUIX.   I'm afraid your wife is as extravagant as she is charming. When I suggest granite for the foyer, she's quick to counter with Peruvian marble. The tapestries she's prescribed for your boudoir are no less than spun gold, and the dining set she fancies is inlaid with bone carved from the antler of a rare species of elk, common only to the Himalayas.

DR. ROYER-COLLARD.   So that's the price she extorts for fealty?

MONSIEUR PROUIX.   Why, the proposed garden alone could bankrupt a man —

DR. ROYER-COLLARD.   Spend what you must.

MONSIEUR PROUIX.   With all due respect, sir, your resources are finite —

DR. ROYER-COLLARD.   I'm well aware of my own finances —

MONSIEUR PROUIX.   Why, even the cost of lumber —

DR. ROYER-COLLARD.   Whatever you require, I'll provide!

MONSIEUR PROUIX.   Pardon me, Doctor, I meant no insult ...

DR. ROYER-COLLARD. More than my marriage is at stake, Monsieur Prouix. If my wife runs rampant here in Saint Maurice, the Ministry will call my very competence into question. I can hear them now. "We've entrusted over five hundred madmen to his care. How can he keep the lunatics at bay, when he can't even harness his own wife?"

MONSIEUR PROUIX. Excuse me for saying it, sir, but I never dreamed a man of your pragmatism and reserve could be so swayed by a woman's influence.

DR. ROYER-COLLARD. She's a rare bird, Monsieur Prouix. I intend to keep her caged. *(From off, a woman's voice.)*

RENÉE PÉLAGIE. *(Off.)* I must see the Doctor at once!

DR. ROYER-COLLARD. What the devil —

MONSIEUR PROUIX. Is that the sound of Duty, calling?

DR. ROYER-COLLARD. It more than calls, Monsieur. It screeches.

RENÉE PÉLAGIE. *(Off.)* It's beyond urgent! It's dire! *(The door swings open, and Renée Pélagie storms in, distraught.)*

Scene 2

Renée Pélagie, Dr. Royer Collard, Monsieur Prouix.

RENÉE PÉLAGIE. I beseech you, Doctor, let me speak!

DR. ROYER-COLLARD. But Madame, I do not even know you. It is customary to write first, requesting an appointment.

RENÉE PÉLAGIE. Desperation has driven me past etiquette, head-long into frenzy!

DR. ROYER-COLLARD. My schedule is not subject to the whims of lunatics.

RENÉE PÉLAGIE. I beg to differ, Doctor. You work in a madhouse. Your every waking moment is governed by the insane.

DR. ROYER-COLLARD. Shall I call for the guard and have you removed?

RENÉE PÉLAGIE. You have a choice. Hear me out, or watch

9

as I curdle and die before you, a victim of my own cancerous grief. Denied its expression, I will surely be poisoned by it, and collapse at your feet, a spent cipher, a corpse. *(Dr. Royer-Collard turns to Monsieur Prouix.)*

DR. ROYER-COLLARD.   Excuse us a moment, won't you, Monsieur Prouix?

MONSIEUR PROUIX.   But of course. *(He withdraws. Dr. Royer-Collard addresses Renée Pélagie.)*

DR. ROYER-COLLARD.   I beg you — be succinct.

RENÉE PÉLAGIE.   I have fallen prey to yet another abomination in this unending Cavalcade of Woe which I am doomed to call "my life."

DR. ROYER-COLLARD.   And how might I assist you?

RENÉE PÉLAGIE.   You are new to Charenton, are you not?

DR. ROYER-COLLARD.   I am.

RENÉE PÉLAGIE.   Perhaps you are not yet familiar with my husband, and his unusual case.

DR. ROYER-COLLARD.   He is a patient here, I presume?

RENÉE PÉLAGIE.   Quite.

DR. ROYER-COLLARD.   His name?

RENÉE PÉLAGIE.   I cannot bring myself to say it, Doctor. Its cost has been so dear. *(She hands a calling card to Dr. Royer-Collard. He reacts:)*

DR. ROYER-COLLARD.   With all due respect, Madame, all of France is familiar with your husband.

RENÉE PÉLAGIE.   No one knows his reputation better than I, Doctor.

DR. ROYER-COLLARD.   I assume that you've come to plead for clemency on his behalf.

RENÉE PÉLAGIE.   Oh you do, do you?

DR. ROYER-COLLARD.   I'm afraid I can offer nothing more than sympathy. I have the strictest orders, in a writ signed by Napoleon himself, to contain the man indefinitely.

RENÉE PÉLAGIE.   It is my dearest hope, Doctor, that he remain entombed forever, that he be deprived all human contact, and that when at last he perishes in the dank bowels of your institution, he be left as carrion for the rodents and the worms.

DR. ROYER-COLLARD.   I stand corrected, Madame.

RENÉE PÉLAGIE.   I have paid in blood, sir, for the mere fact I am his wife, and he my husband.

DR. ROYER-COLLARD.   I see ...

RENÉE PÉLAGIE.   I don't know which has plagued me more. His grotesque résumé of crimes, or their notoriety. When he mutilated that poor beggar, her backside forked through like a pastry shell, no one was more mortified than I. His orgy in the school yard — those pitiful children, that lethal pox — well, it rent the fabric of my heart. *But I was no less moved when, on a country weekend in Chambéry, our hostess, upon learning I was his spouse, spat a mouthful of Côtes du Rhone upon my breast.* In that moment, all his cruelties coalesced into the single liquid projectile issuing from her lips.

DR. ROYER-COLLARD.   Ironic as it may seem, moral outrage often finds its expression in coarse gesture.

RENÉE PÉLAGIE.   Everywhere I go, the same scenario ensues! The other evening, at the opera, I was seated in my box, a few scant meters from the stage. In the midst of her aria, the soprano spotted my face in the crowd. She stopped, midnote. The orchestra ceased its play, and the diva cried, "Look! Here in our midst, *Satan's bride!*" Slowly, a thousand opera glasses turned to stare in my direction. I bolted to the door. Stricken, I hauled myself into the nearest church. There, I pleaded for absolution from my husband's sins. When I left, the very pew in which I sat was yanked from the floor by a trio of priests, and carried into the courtyard. There, as they intoned the sacred rite of exorcism, they burned the very wood I had sullied with my behind! *(She dissolves into a spasm of tears.)* Oh, Doctor, forgive my hysteria, but I am a woman plagued!

DR. ROYER-COLLARD.   Careful Marquise! Women who take to screaming in these hallways often land themselves in leg irons.

RENÉE PÉLAGIE.   I am no stranger to such contraptions, Doctor.

DR. ROYER-COLLARD.   You, too, fell prey to his appetites?

RENÉE PÉLAGIE.   It's as though my body were his conscience in corporeal form, scarred beyond all repair.

11

DR. ROYER-COLLARD. What specifically compelled you to pay this visit today? *(Renée Pélagie composes herself.)*
RENÉE PÉLAGIE.   I dared hope that my husband's incarceration would allow him to fade from the country's memory. I could then find freedom in his obscurity. Oh, to take tea again! To be invited on a garden stroll! To once again know the unfettered glory of walking down the street without insult. Without falling debris.
DR. ROYER-COLLARD.   I wish it for you, my poor Marquise.
RENÉE PÉLAGIE.   But something prevents this happy turn of events.
DR. ROYER-COLLARD.   What, exactly?
RENÉE PÉLAGIE.   Are you aware, sir, of the charge which precipitated my husband's latest arrest?
DR. ROYER-COLLARD.   I am. He authored a scandalous novel. A tale so pornographic, that it drove men to murder, and women to miscarry.
RENÉE PÉLAGIE.   And are you further aware, that now — even within these fortified chambers — his writing continues, unchecked?
DR. ROYER-COLLARD.   What?
RENÉE PÉLAGIE.   Charenton provides a haven most agreeable to his Muse. Endless hours to write, without interruption, save for his meals. Stacks of paper at his disposal, rivers of ink, and always — *always* — a ready quill.
DR. ROYER-COLLARD.   I assure you, Madame, this is the first I have heard of such goings-on.
RENÉE PÉLAGIE.   I thought my husband had been placed here at Charenton, in lieu of prison, so that he could be cured of his corrosive habits.
DR. ROYER-COLLARD.   I recognize our failing. I even know its cause.
RENÉE PÉLAGIE.   Yes?
DR. ROYER-COLLARD.   It pains me to admit that our reputation is one of laxity. A certain Abbe de Coulmier, administrator here, has a constitution more suited to nursing babies than tending the insane. He has removed the wicker dummy, the wire cage, and the straitjacket — tools many consider es-

sential to our trade — and replaced them with musical inter-
ludes, watercolor exercises, even Marivaux.

RENÉE PÉLAGIE.   I had no idea that art offered salvation
from madness. I was of the opinion that most artists are, themselves, quite deranged.

DR. ROYER-COLLARD.   That is the very reason the Ministry
has named me to this post. To enforce a more stringent at-
mosphere.

RENÉE PÉLAGIE.   I pray that for your sake and mine, you
succeed at your assigned task. *(A pause. Dr. Royer-Collard frowns.)*

DR. ROYER-COLLARD.   It's not so easily done, Madame. We
require blacksmiths, to cast new shackles. A battalion of guards.
Thumbscrews and pillories, to keep the patients tranquil. I'm
afraid our resources are already strained.

RENÉE PÉLAGIE.   That is your worry, sir, not mine.

DR. ROYER-COLLARD.   On the contrary, Madame. If you
were to buttress your entreaties with, perhaps, the means to
oblige them ...

RENÉE PÉLAGIE.   I am not a wealthy woman.

DR. ROYER-COLLARD.   Your husband's legal records routinely cross this desk. Is it not true, that the recent sale of his
mansion at La Coste has granted you a sudden windfall?

RENÉE PÉLAGIE.   A trifling nest egg, hardly a fortune.

DR. ROYER-COLLARD.   If you are truly determined to step
out of the long, dark shadow of your husband's celebrity ...

RENÉE PÉLAGIE.   Oh, but I am!

DR. ROYER-COLLARD.   Words alone are insufficient.

RENÉE PÉLAGIE.   It's beyond perversity. That honor should
carry a price-tag!

DR. ROYER-COLLARD.   Picture it. A summer's picnic, linens strewn, an array of succulents, old friends once again
deigning to kiss your hand. "Why, Marquise! Enchanted to see
you! Welcome back from your long, dark descent into the
abyss of infamy!"

RENÉE PÉLAGIE.   Don't toy with me Doctor!

DR. ROYER-COLLARD.   Now is the time to secure your epi-
taph. Renée Pélagie de Montreuil ... or *"Satan's Bride."* *(A tor-
turous moment for Renée Pélagie.)*

13

RENÉE PÉLAGIE.   Name it, and the figure shall be yours.
DR. ROYER-COLLARD.   Might I suggest, Madame, that we keep our new-found understanding in confidence.
RENÉE PÉLAGIE.   Of course.
DR. ROYER-COLLARD.   Far be it from me to press the matter ...
RENÉE PÉLAGIE.   You may expect my lawyer later this afternoon. I trust that, together, you'll arrive at a commensurate sum.
DR. ROYER-COLLARD.   I'm eternally in your debt.
RENÉE PÉLAGIE.   And I in yours. *(She turns to go; she turns back to Dr. Royer-Collard:)* Doctor?
DR. ROYER-COLLARD.   Marquise?
RENÉE PÉLAGIE.   Can I impart to you his cruelest trick?
DR. ROYER-COLLARD.   Yes.
RENÉE PÉLAGIE.   Once ... long ago ... in the folly of youth ... he made me ... *love him.*
DR. ROYER-COLLARD.   My sympathies, Madame.
RENÉE PÉLAGIE.   Tell me truthfully. Will my maligned character, stretched so long upon the rack of ignominy, ever regain its natural shape?
DR. ROYER-COLLARD.   Take heart! *(He kisses Renée Pélagie's hand.)* How suddenly such happiness looms!

Scene 3

Dr. Royer-Collard, Abbe de Coulmier, The Marquis.

DR. ROYER-COLLARD.   The Ministry informs me that The Marquis falls under your exclusive dominion.
COULMIER.   My brethren found him too taxing a patient. A few of the priests were so dispirited, they left the order. Father Lely now slaughters pigs in Provence. Father Couvrat is a chimney sweep. And the late Father Buffier is rumored to

have buried himself alive rather than minister to The Marquis, in hopes of achieving martyrdom through less rigorous means.

DR. ROYER-COLLARD. And you?

COULMIER. I welcome the challenge.

DR. ROYER-COLLARD. Tell me, what is The Marquis' current regimen?

COULMIER. Ample rest, seclusion, a frigid bath, and twice a week he takes the vapors.

DR. ROYER-COLLARD. He has never once been bled, consigned to the pit, borne the weight of the iron mask?

COULMIER. Forgive my impertinence, Doctor, but you are a learned man, so perhaps you can enlighten me: how can inhumane treatment produce a civilized demeanor? The methods you cite are no less than medieval; I would not visit them upon a dog.

DR. ROYER-COLLARD. And the effect of your preferred prescriptions?

COULMIER. The Marquis no longer roars or spits. He no longer scarifies his skin. His appetite is solid, and his sleep sound.

DR. ROYER-COLLARD. And his prose?

COULMIER. Even a man in the most advanced stages of mental decay is, I believe, still entitled to a modicum of privacy. While I permit him the privilege of his writing exercises, I do not take it upon myself to read them.

DR. ROYER-COLLARD. And yet it seems they might provide the surest barometer of his progress.

COULMIER. Given his new-found docility and reserve, I wouldn't be surprised if his prose — once ripe with the stench of indecency — now borders on the liturgical.

DR. ROYER-COLLARD. A generous supposition.

COULMIER. He is a walking placard for humanitarian strategies in our hospitals, our asylums, even — I'll posit — our Bastilles.

DR. ROYER-COLLARD. Then I'm sure you won't take offense when I tell you that — to affirm his recovery — I requested a thorough search of The Marquis' quarters.

COULMIER. The results, I trust, were unexceptional.

DR. ROYER-COLLARD.   Quite the contrary. It yielded some alarming contraband. *(He gestures to the items on his desk.)* Two razors, a purse filled with salt, a wooden prod, newly greased, and a small, iron vice-grip of indeterminate usage.
COULMIER.   I am no less than stunned, Doctor.
DR. ROYER-COLLARD.   These knick-knacks are of minimal concern, since they pose no threat to the Asylum's general population. However, stashed under a floorboard, we recovered this. *(He pulls a sheath of papers from his desk.)* A manuscript, some twelve hundred pages long, ready for printing.
COULMIER.   Another? So soon? *(Dr. Royer-Collard passes the manuscript to Coulmier.)*
DR. ROYER-COLLARD.   I defy you — in the name of God, France, and all that you hold moral and true — to read it, unmoved. *(Coulmier begins to read it. Lights rise on the opposite side of the stage, revealing The Marquis, seated in his quarters. His hair is elaborately coifed, and his ruffles are somewhat worn. He writes, quill in hand, reciting as he works.)*
THE MARQUIS.   Dear Reader, it now falls upon me, your chaperone through the dark waters of the soul, to impart a tale of such mirthless cruelty and moral torpor that I can barely bring my voice above a whisper. So come, perch upon my knee, so you don't miss a word. *(He giggles. Coulmier glances nervously at Dr. Royer-Collard.)*
DR. ROYER-COLLARD.   Gird yourself. That's mere preamble.
(Coulmier continues to read.)
THE MARQUIS.   On a jutting cliff outside the city of Marseilles, there stood a monastery of most sinister design. To the gullible eye, its windowless facade suggested a simplicity well-suited to modest worship. But the true reason for its austerity was far graver — to conceal from the world at large the atrocities occurring within. *(He spins his tale with all the unfettered glee of a mischievous child inventing a lie. He registers delight at each grisly escapade, giddiness at each perversion.)* It was here our young hero first sprang into the world, borne of a defrocked priest, and a wayward nun. Once the baby was freed from its mother's sin-ripened womb, its parents were duly skewered for their offenses. Bereft and wailing, the child was

16

alone. His only parent was the church, his only playmates its grim practitioners. Soon, he blossomed into boyhood. On his chin, soft down, and between the orbs of his dimpled ass, a blushing rosebud begging to be ... plucked. Would that he were carrion before vultures! Would that he were a quivering faun trapped in a lion's gaze! *Would that he were anything but a comely boy surrounded by priests!*

COULMIER.   I can smell its incipient odor, Doctor.

DR. ROYER-COLLARD.   What's that, Abbe?

COULMIER.   Blasphemy. The last refuge of the failed provocateur.

DR. ROYER-COLLARD.   Just wait. He brings new vigor to an old standard.

THE MARQUIS.   So great was his beauty, so pungent was his youth, that the black-robed friars had christened him with the name "Ganymede." The youth soon became unsurpassed in the field of debauchery. Oh, dear Reader, what evils a man can commit when reason demurs to lust! For these were Ganymede's teachers: an aged Monk so withered and limp that frottage was his highest aspiration; an Arch Bishop whose aperture was so fetid and of such slack diameter that it resembled the seat of an untended privy more than any human hole — *(Coulmier swoons, dabbing at his brow.)*

COULMIER.   Look at me; I'm awash in perspiration.

THE MARQUIS.   A lapsed Prelate who, when Ganymede felt Nature's rustlings, insisted that he use his gaping maw as its receptacle —

COULMIER.   Heaven forfend!

THE MARQUIS.   And most atrociously, a Viennese Cardinal and his participatory horse.

COULMIER.   Participatory?

DR. ROYER-COLLARD.   Picture it!

COULMIER.   Nature herself was never more abused!

THE MARQUIS.   Ganymede weathered these requests with the cool detachment of one already dulled by life's demands. He had no time to pursue the twin luxuries of Faith and Piety; his only aim was to survive. And to do so, he knew he must offer his flesh, naked on a plate, for the frantic lapping of a hundred unholy tongues. This is what a life spent in the bosom of the Church had taught him …

DR. ROYER-COLLARD.   Endless pages of philosophy follow. *(Coulmier begins frantically flipping through the pages.)*

THE MARQUIS.   — No God — blah, blah — dominion through force — blah, blah — the inevitability of chaos — blah, blah, blah —

COULMIER.   But what of the boy's fate?

DR. ROYER-COLLARD.   Swept away by the story, are you?

COULMIER.   It's necessary to know his end, to gauge the full measure of The Marquis' depravity.

DR. ROYER-COLLARD.   Page seventy-three. I've folded the corner. *(Coulmier regards Dr. Royer-Collard for a moment.)*

THE MARQUIS.   Soon Ganymede was adopted by the Duc de Blangis, a rank old pedophile with a penchant for gutter trade. "What soft skin you have!" cooed the Duc, when the boy lay exposed before him. "So womanish! So suitable for lechery! I will not have it wrinkle or coarsen; rather, I'll preserve its sheen forever!" With that, the Duc uncorked a vial of linseed oil. He dribbled it over the child's nude body, filling each crevice, each moist valley, till Ganymede shone like an eel. Then he wrapped the boy in freshly harvested donkey hide. "Here you'll stay," the Duc commanded, "until you've absorbed each drop. Only then will we commence with our debauch!" Accustomed to the most vile abuses, the boy found such treatment a happy respite. The hide was warm and soft, and daily the Duc fed him the most astonishing foods. Marzipan, hot sugared pastries, cream-filled cakes and glacés. "Mon Dieu," sighed the boy, "I could live this life forever!" Soon, however, Ganymede realized the appalling truth.

COULMIER.   What cruel twist has The Marquis in store?

THE MARQUIS.   The calculating Duc had not cured the enveloping hide, and so — as the boy's body, gorged with desserts, grew swollen like a great, pink bladder — its casing began to shrink.

COULMIER.   Dear God!

THE MARQUIS.   "Please," beseeched the boy, "Split the hide, so I might breathe free!" The Duc merely laughed, and si-

lenced his victim with a few spoonfuls of mousse. The boy
could suffocate or swallow, so swallow he did, increasing his
girth and thereby increasing his torment. Soon, the child was
prepared to strike any bargain. "Free me from this leather
prison, and you can use me as your slave!" "Don't you see,
little one?" purred the Duc. "My delectation has already begun." In time, Ganymede's back arched in a circle, and his
shoulders met. He felt his rib cage close upon itself, like a
lady's purse, snapped shut at the opera. With that, the Duc
de Blangis released his loins, the hot-seed of his tumescence
spiraling through the air like molten lava from some belch-
ing volcano —

COULMIER. ENOUGH! *(The Marquis shrugs; the lights on him
fade.)*

DR. ROYER-COLLARD. That's only the first chapter.

COULMIER. Already he's catalogued every known vice —
and some hitherto unknown!

DR. ROYER-COLLARD. And that page is followed by eleven
hundred and fifty-seven more.

COULMIER. Astonishing.

DR. ROYER-COLLARD. Imagine if this wound its way among
the inmates.

COULMIER. I'd sooner introduce a match to tinder.

DR. ROYER-COLLARD. This man is licentious. *Turpitudinous.*

COULMIER. And *prolific!*

DR. ROYER-COLLARD. And to think, only moments ago,
you labeled him a triumph of rehabilitation.

COULMIER. I'm driven to distrust my own capacity for judgment.

DR. ROYER-COLLARD. You treat him like a man, Abbe;
therein lies your error. In faculties, he's nothing but an er-
rant child. Each time you coddle him, you invite more of his
dark mischief. Don't you see? He's all but begging to be
strung up by the toes.

COULMIER. It chills me to think, sir, that our institution
might perpetuate the very horrors The Marquis himself so
painstakingly describes.

DR. ROYER-COLLARD. What is most reassuring to the lu-

natic? The sight of the shackles, waiting for him. It's like a balm to his uneasy mind; in them, he sees the architecture of all civilization.
COULMIER.   I implore you, do not insist that I negate my principles. Let me continue in my charitable course.
DR. ROYER-COLLARD.   Understand that his reformation is an urgent priority.
COULMIER.   I'll do all that I can.
DR. ROYER-COLLARD.   Do more. Otherwise, I'll be forced to report to the Ministry that the inmates are indeed running the asylum.

Scene 4

Madeleine, The Marquis.

MADELEINE.   I've darned your stockings, and the hem on your nightdress.
THE MARQUIS.   I won't wear them, Madeleine. Never again, my little rosette, my pearl ...
MADELEINE.   Don't start, you filthy old goat.
THE MARQUIS.   I'll enshrine them in my closet, knowing it was your fingers which drove the needle through their membranes!
MADELEINE.   Some day, I'll use that same needle to sew your mouth shut.
THE MARQUIS.   Promises, promises!
MADELEINE.   I'm allowed to collect a few extra louis. When it's personal effects I'm repairing. *(The Marquis gives her some change.)*
THE MARQUIS.   Would that these coins purchased your other talents, too!
MADELEINE.   That's not all. There's something else I want from you.
THE MARQUIS.   You've already stolen my heart, as well as another more prominent organ, south of the Equator ...

MADELEINE.   Mother says I'm not to leave without a story.

THE MARQUIS.   A voracious reader, your mother.

MADELEINE.   She's stone blind, on account of all the lye in the laundry kettles. Soaking sheets for lunatics cost the poor lady her sight. I read 'em to her.

THE MARQUIS.   Oh?

MADELEINE.   Every night about eight, we sit at the table, and I start in reciting, from wherever it was we left it the night before. Sometimes, when it's a beheading, or some broken thing is locked in a dungeon, crying for the loss of her chastity, my mother's face goes pale, she sets down her glass and she says —

THE MARQUIS.   Yes?

MADELEINE.   "Read that part again!"

THE MARQUIS.   Nothing like a good tingle, is there, Madeleine?

MADELEINE.   Sometimes I have to slam the book shut, just to catch my breath. Mama turns all a-twitter, cranky for the delay, and makes me forge on ...

THE MARQUIS.   When the priests taught you to read, did they foresee your taste in novels?

MADELEINE.   You're not the only one, mind you. We read Monsieur de Laclos, and Louvet de Couvray. "But when we want a good scare," says Mama, "make it The Marquis!"

THE MARQUIS.   Do I frighten you now, Madeleine?

MADELEINE.   You? Frighten me? That's a good one! I tell Mama, "If you could only see him, you wouldn't tremble so at his tales. Who'd have thought such a spent body could still boast such a fertile mind?"

THE MARQUIS.   That's the only frontier I have left, dearest. And what kind of story shall it be tonight?

MADELEINE.   Something to make our blood run cold, and set our cheeks aflame.

THE MARQUIS.   Just how bad would you like it to be?

MADELEINE.   Past all redemption, please.

THE MARQUIS.   I have just the manuscript, inspired by these very surroundings. The unhappy tale of a virginal nurse-maid, the darling of the lower wards, where they entomb the hopelessly deranged.

MADELEINE. Is it awfully violent?

THE MARQUIS. Most assuredly.

MADELEINE. Is it terribly erotic?

THE MARQUIS. Fiendishly so!

MADELEINE. Is it both at once?

THE MARQUIS. But of course!

MADELEINE. Ooh, that sounds like a fine one!

THE MARQUIS. But it comes with a price. *(He holds up the manuscript.)* A kiss for each page.

MADELEINE. My, that's steep.

THE MARQUIS. There are, of course, lesser authors waiting to be read …

MADELEINE. Must I administer the kisses directly, or might I blow them?

THE MARQUIS. The price, my coquette, is as firm as my javelin.

MADELEINE. Oh, you! You talk same as you write. *(She sighs, then kisses The Marquis. He gives her a page. She kisses him again. Another page. A third time, a third page.)* It's a long story, this one.

THE MARQUIS. And this — the climax of the story — comes at a higher cost!

MADELEINE. What's that then?

THE MARQUIS. Sit on my lap.

MADELEINE. *(Madeleine mutters as she crawls into his lap:)* You demand a lot from your readers, you do.

THE MARQUIS. Needless to say, the story's thrilling conclusion comes at a premium.

MADELEINE. What would that be, pray tell?

THE MARQUIS. *(The Marquis whispers in her ear, his tone low and hypnotic.)* Your maidenhead. And then you must turn your needle and thread upon yourself. Sew it up as tightly as when you were a virgin, and come back to me, renewed, so I can deflower it a second time. *(Madeleine stares at him a moment, stunned. Suddenly, she slaps him, hard.)*

MADELEINE. Some things belong on paper, others in life. It's a blessed fool who can't tell the difference. *(Coulmier ap-*

pears. He observes The Marquis and Madeleine, entangled. He clears his throat.)
COULMIER.   Mademoiselle Leclerc.
MADELEINE.   You're in the nick of it, Abbe. This old lech forgot himself for a moment. He thought I was a character in one of his nasty books. *(Madeleine thrusts her tongue out at The Marquis, and exits.)*

Scene 5

Coulmier, The Marquis.

COULMIER.   It is those same books which have precipitated my visit, dear Marquis. *(The Marquis uncorks a decanter.)*
THE MARQUIS.   Care for a splash of wine, Abbe?
COULMIER.   Here? Now? It's not yet noon.
THE MARQUIS.   Conversation, like certain portions of the anatomy, always runs more smoothly when lubricated.
COULMIER.   Why, yes, thank-you. *(The Marquis pours two glasses of wine.)*
THE MARQUIS.   It's a rare vintage, from an obscure village in Bordeaux. Rather than crush the grape underfoot, they place the fruit on the belly of a bride, and reap its juices when the young husband steers his vessel into port.
COULMIER.   Oh, my.
THE MARQUIS.   Swish it gently in the glass before tasting. You can smell the perfume in her hair, and the beads of sweat from that nether region called Love's Temple. A full-bodied flavor with just a hint of wantonness? *(Coulmier stops mid-draught, coughs, and sets his glass down.)*
COULMIER.   As you know, most esteemed Marquis, the staff has done its utmost to render you comfortable here.
THE MARQUIS.   It's true, dear-heart, you've spoiled me pink.
COULMIER.   A canopied bed, in lieu of a straw mat. An ample library, including the latest medical volumes, as per your

request. A settee of yellow Utrecht velvet, and a portrait of your very own father, painted in miniature upon an ivory horn, and ... lest we forget ... a well stocked supply of paper, with enough quills to feather an ostrich.

THE MARQUIS.   For these, I am most grateful.

COULMIER.   We are delighted that Charenton so readily invokes your muse.

THE MARQUIS.   Stories tumble from me here faster than I can record them.

COULMIER.   This has not escaped our attention. Pleased though I may be at your prolificity — I'm afraid I have to place certain censures upon your quill, dear Marquis.

THE MARQUIS.   Not content to be my jailer, you're now my editor as well?

COULMIER.   From this moment forward, I beseech you, for your own good as well as mine — no more ribald tales!

THE MARQUIS.   You didn't care for my little Ganymede.

COULMIER.   No.

THE MARQUIS.   But you read about his exploits nonetheless.

COULMIER.   Yes.

THE MARQUIS.   By candlelight you licked the words off the paper, and rolled them around in your mouth. You swallowed. You succumbed.

COULMIER.   My interest was professional, sir, not prurient.

THE MARQUIS.   Did you read every word? Or did you run straight away to the dog-eared pages?

COULMIER.   Enough to discern the novel's tenor.

THE MARQUIS.   And — ?

COULMIER.   It stirred in me a most pressing desire.

THE MARQUIS.   To copulate?

COULMIER.   To bathe. It's offensive, in every realm. A compendium of perversities.

THE MARQUIS.   Surely, if such phenomena exist in nature, then they are fair game in fiction ...

COULMIER.   You expect me to believe that these atrocities occur?

THE MARQUIS.   We don't run in the same circles, do we,

24

my cherub?

COULMIER.   I work in a madhouse. Still I've never seen any-thing such as you describe.

THE MARQUIS.   If they can be dreamt, they can be done.

COULMIER.   Permit me, for a moment, to play the role of critic, dear Marquis. Morally, your tale has a smug tone, con-demning its principals while delighting in their misbehavior. It purports to advocate virtue by detailing vice. At best, a wob-bly proposition.

THE MARQUIS.   Why must morality serve as the book's ba-rometer? It's an entertainment, my persimmon; not a moral treatise.

COULMIER.   But — in a world too often governed by man's fickle tastes — morality is our only bedrock. It is the golden standard against which we are all judged.

THE MARQUIS.   But that's preposterous! Morality is a con-venience, nothing more!

COULMIER.   Surely a man so oft afoul of the law is more cognizant of its boundaries.

THE MARQUIS.   There was a time, my love, when I was brought to trial for the depucilating of seven very young girls. Mind you, all I did was spoon them diuretics — the other charges were hysterical. Nevertheless, I was sentenced to the Bastille. The judge blamed my behavior on my Noble birth. "You aristocrats," he bellowed, "feasting on the helpless, nour-ishing your vices on the spoils of the poor! Soon, the worm will turn!" *Well!* When the Bastille was stormed and liberated by the mob, they told me I was one of their own! "Impover-ished slave," they cried, "Puppet of the Ruling Class! Let us reward your suffering with freedom!" Who, I implore you, was right? The judge? The mob? One insisted I was a perpetra-tor, the other, a victim. Each claimed it was a matter of *moral principle.* What in this story is constant? Some abstract moral-ity, applied to the tatters of my tiny life? I think not! *Only me!* Only me and those seven little girls, left to spend eternity evacuating in the loo …

COULMIER.   You risk offending more than man; you risk offending God.

THE MARQUIS. Oh, please!

COULMIER. Theologically, your story is utterly damning; Ganymede borne of the union between two lapsed celibates. His parents are more Dionysian than Catholic; they make a mockery of their chastity vows.

THE MARQUIS. It's chastity vows that make a mockery of men. My Uncle, the Abbe de Sade, was esteemed by his betters in the Church. Yet routinely, he kept one trollop in the confessional, one in the sacristy, and one — naked and squealing — under the baptismal font! That way, between each Sunday Mass, there was always a ready sheath for his sword! Once — and this, my adorable Coulmier, turns even my cheeks to a rosy hue — he administered communion with a harlot under his robes! While he poured Christ's blood into its silver chalice and drank, she imbibed a liquid no less divine!

COULMIER. I fear, Marquis, that sacrilege comes as naturally to you in conversation as it does upon the page.

THE MARQUIS. An atheist cannot be sacrilegious. The word does not exist in his vocabulary. Sacrilege is the exclusive province of the Devout.

COULMIER. Men like your Uncle may fail the Bible, but that hardly merits dismissing its precepts.

THE MARQUIS. But Darling, my novel does not ascribe to the Bible's precepts, and — as such — it should not be held to them in your critique.

COULMIER. How, then, should I evaluate it? As political allegory, perhaps? All right then. It's simplistic and panders to popular sentiment. Ganymede as France, borne the bastard child of the church, indulged by the decadent bourgeoisie, gorged with all manner of useless opulence, until at last his own body revolts against him ...

THE MARQUIS. Where does the novel profess to be a political tract?

COULMIER. What, then, does it desire to be?

THE MARQUIS. LITERATURE, MY PET!

COULMIER. Frankly, it even fails as an exercise in craft. Note the tireless repetition of the words "nipple" and "pikestaff."

THE MARQUIS. There I was taxed; it's true.

COULMIER. The narrative itself is little more than an exhaustive list of mayhems, sans character, sans theme. And such puny scope! Where are its heroes? Its virtues and triumphs?

THE MARQUIS. Must we record only those phenomena that ennoble us as creatures? What unites us, my precious? Common language? A universal God? Shared codes of law and conduct? No. These vary from one population to the next. Fads and habits, nothing more! Did you know, heavenly man, that in France a husband with six wives would be executed, while in darkest Borneo that same man would be crowned king?

COULMIER. But surely there are verities which exceed geography!

THE MARQUIS. Yes! Primal desire — that's unchanging! Every man from Paris to China feels the same urgent stirring in his loins.

COULMIER. Lust is our only denominator?

THE MARQUIS. Of course not!

COULMIER. Pray tell, what other constants do you cite?

THE MARQUIS. We eat, we shit, we kill and we die.

COULMIER. Your selectivity confirms your contrary nature. We are also born, we fall in love, we give birth. May I suggest that you endeavor to write a new novel which embraces those verities?

THE MARQUIS. Man's already deluded himself into believing those illusions underlie his life; why does he need a novel to further them?

COULMIER. Not only would it prove more felicitous to its readers, but it might perform a cathartic function upon its author.

THE MARQUIS. How so, my dear?

COULMIER. It might assuage your libertine dementia. Your current prose only aggravates it.

THE MARQUIS. If Mother Nature didn't want me to tickle my own fancy, she would not have provided me with two industrious hands. I write with one, leaving the other palm free to enjoy the fruits of the first.

COULMIER. He who lives in darkness cowers in the light,

while he who lives in the sun radiates it. Step into the sun for a while, Marquis.

THE MARQUIS.   Permit me to extend your metaphor.

COULMIER.   Be my guest.

THE MARQUIS.   He who sits in the sun is often blinded by it. Then, vulnerable and incognizant, he is devoured by the forces of darkness. Better to stare the fuckers in the face, yes?

COULMIER.   And therein lies the path to Happiness?

THE MARQUIS.   Therein lies survival.

COULMIER.   I hope you won't take offense if I suggest that you reject happiness because you fear it is beyond your reach.

THE MARQUIS.   My lamb! My beguiling young fool! You're not the man to counsel me in happiness or its pursuit.

COULMIER.   Why not? I am content.

THE MARQUIS.   Happiness for you, my little kumquat, is achieved through strict adhesion to Society's mandates. Most men follow this hackneyed passage; like eager children set loose on a scavenger hunt, they dart about in search of the assigned baubles — wives, offspring, gainful employ, handsome homes — and, when they have accrued them all — voila! The promised treasure is won — Happiness ensues! But for me, happiness springs from a different course.

COULMIER.   Which is — ?

THE MARQUIS.   To slice through social artifice, shatter her false conventions, and become one with Nature's Cimmerian Tide, where only the ruthless excel, and where brute force yields its own treasure! Past etiquette, past decency, past morals — that's where happiness lies, like the winking chasm buried deep in the briars of a woman's groin.

COULMIER.   It's true, is it not Marquis, that most of your adult life has been spent in prison?

THE MARQUIS.   My past addresses read like a Primer in Crime. Vincennes, the Madelonettes, Saint Lazare and the Bastille …

COULMIER.   And it was in such a milieu that you first wielded your pen?

THE MARQUIS.   Oh, my angel! Hell itself is the crucible in which I forged my craft. From the Citadel at Picpus, I could see the gallows. Day after day during the Terror, I watched the endless procession to the chopping block. Heads, like champagne corks, flying. My only music was the sound of grief. Its melody was the wretched crying of widows and orphaned children; its percussion, the steady rhythm of the falling blade; its bass, the thud of the cadavers as they rolled down the bank into the pit below. Blood flowed in rivers beneath my window, Abbe.

COULMIER.   Perhaps it's best not to extrapolate man's character from such surroundings.

THE MARQUIS.   Where better? There, stripped of all postures, man's true self surges to the fore!

COULMIER.   You've left me no choice. *(He pauses, then says resolutely:)* I'm afraid I have to confiscate your paper, and your quill.

THE MARQUIS.   What?

COULMIER.   You heard me.

THE MARQUIS.   But they're all I have!

COULMIER.   We cure the drunkard by seizing his liquor. We cure the glutton by absconding with his meal. We cure the rapist by castration.

THE MARQUIS.   I can weather your reviews, but spare me this!

COULMIER.   We must assuage these perverse fantasies.

THE MARQUIS.   But don't you agree that my only salvation is to vent them on paper?

COULMIER.   Have you considered reading to pass the hours? A writer who produces more than he reads — the sure mark of an amateur.

THE MARQUIS.   My writing is involuntary, like the beating of my heart! My constant erection! I CAN'T HELP IT!

COULMIER.   Then we shall stop it for you.

THE MARQUIS.   Why? Because I don't cater to the moment's tastes?

COULMIER.   Because your novels are a symptom of your insanity.

THE MARQUIS.   On the contrary — they keep me sane!

COULMIER.   I am sorry. Truly.

THE MARQUIS. I'll write dainty stories then! Odes to Virtue!
COULMIER. I'll have Valcour collect the items in question.
THE MARQUIS. What of my faithful readers?
COULMIER. You've written enough for one lifetime.
THE MARQUIS. What of the little seamstress?
COULMIER. She'd do well to steer clear of your influence.
THE MARQUIS. I have a proposition!
COULMIER. You always do.
THE MARQUIS. She's a luscious morsel, Madeleine. What pulsates beneath those skirts is worth succor! I'm certain I could convince her of the benefits inherent in granting favors to a superior ...
COULMIER. I don't know who you insult more: her or me.
THE MARQUIS. THEN BUGGER ME!
COULMIER. Don't make me ill ...
THE MARQUIS. YOU CAN PLUNDER EVERY PORE, AND LOB MY KNOB BESIDES! ANYTHING!
COULMIER. Good day, Monsieur. (*He heads for the door. The Marquis drops his desperate pose, and coos.*)
THE MARQUIS. Oh, Cupid. My little minx ...
COULMIER. Yes?
THE MARQUIS. Where there's a will, there's a way. And a maniac is matchless for invention.

Scene 6

Dr. Royer-Collard, Monsieur Prouix

DR. ROYER-COLLARD. Ah! Monsieur Prouix! And how is my new house faring?
MONSIEUR PROUIX. I've come to thank you for loosening your purse-strings. The rather dramatic increase in funds behooves us both.
DR. ROYER-COLLARD. It better. I've been forced to devise the most creative financing imaginable ...
MONSIEUR PROUIX. Your chateau shall undoubtedly be my

masterwork!

DR. ROYER-COLLARD. Yours is an enviable profession, Monsieur Prouix.

MONSIEUR PROUIX. Mine, sir?

DR. ROYER-COLLARD. Yes indeed. You fabricate the design — each plank, each joist, each pilaster — but you leave the execution to others. Your own grand plan is put into action ... and you never hoist a stone, or drive a nail. That's the true measure of a man's authority, isn't it?

MONSIEUR PROUIX. Well, sir. When you put it that way —

DR. ROYER-COLLARD. Is my wife pleased with your progress?

MONSIEUR PROUIX. Yesterday, the silk brocade arrived for the walls of her toilette. She was in the throes of delight. Did you know, sir, that her eyes match its color? I flatter myself that the chateau shall be a tribute to her beauty; its golden cornices, the hue of her hair. Its alabaster stone, the tint of her bosom. Its portals, spread ever wide, as frank and inviting as her very nature ... *(Coulmier enters.)*

COULMIER. Pardon me, Doctor, but I was summoned at your behest.

DR. ROYER-COLLARD. Yes of course. Monsieur Prouix. You'll have to complete your little rhapsody another time.

MONSIEUR PROUIX. Happily sir. Your servant, sir. *(Monsieur Prouix backs out of the room, bowing.)*

Scene 7

Dr. Royer-Collard, Coulmier, Madeleine, The Marquis.

COULMIER. I'm sorry to interrupt, Doctor, but your missive had an urgent tone.

DR. ROYER-COLLARD. A curious phenomenon has beset Charenton. It seems that the bed sheets, curtains and towels — usually so pristine — have acquired of late a burgundy tincture. Some of the patients find this most distressing. Accus-

31

tomed to more sterile hues, they now find themselves bathed in scarlet. It unsettles them.

COULMIER.   Surely its the fault of the laundress, Madame Leclerc. She's quite blind; perhaps her kettles are stained with rust.

DR. ROYER-COLLARD.   Our little mystery has a more engrossing denouement. I spoke this morning with Madame Leclerc's daughter, Madeleine. *(Lights rise on Madeleine.)*

MADELEINE.   I swear I don't know, sir. But it's rather a lovely shade, if I do say so.

DR. ROYER-COLLARD.   You realize, of course, that this casts aspersions upon your mother's skills. After all … a blind laundress. Would you hire a crippled dancer, or a pianist without hands?

MADELEINE.   She's a devoted woman, who, in spite of the afflictions its caused her, stays by her job.

DR. ROYER-COLLARD.   You're a spirited girl, aren't you, Madeleine? You would defend your mother to the core?

MADELEINE.   I would, sir.

DR. ROYER-COLLARD.   And you realize, of course, that to withhold any pertinent information regarding her laxity could cost you both your tenure here?

MADELEINE.   You'd sack us then?

DR. ROYER-COLLARD.   Precisely.

MADELEINE.   Please, sir! Cast me out upon the street, and I'd survive. But my poor Mother! Without her sight, and hardly a tooth in her head, she'd soon be dead. And who's to pay for burial? At least here we're guaranteed a pit alongside the morons.

DR. ROYER-COLLARD.   Now … fully appraised of the situation … would you care to amend your earlier statement? *(Madeleine pauses. For an excruciating moment, she weighs her options. Then, a resolute answer.)*

MADELEINE.   No, Monsieur.

DR. ROYER-COLLARD.   You are certain.

MADELEINE.   I am.

DR. ROYER-COLLARD.   Very well. You and yours are to vacate the premises no later than —

MADELEINE. But Monsieur —

DR. ROYER-COLLARD.   — no later than noon, at which time —

MADELEINE. It was The Marquis!

DR. ROYER-COLLARD. The Marquis?

MADELEINE. Relieved of paper and pen, but not the urge to write, he took to his linens!

DR. ROYER-COLLARD. What?

MADELEINE. He wrote his stories on bed sheets, penning them with the wine from his evening meal. His words bled into the fibers of the cloth.

DR. ROYER-COLLARD. And the nature of these bed-time tales ...

MADELEINE. Silly froth, mostly.

DR. ROYER-COLLARD. Can you be more explicit?

MADELEINE. Than The Marquis? Never!

DR. ROYER-COLLARD. If ever there was a time to humor me, Miss Leclerc, it is now.

MADELEINE. It was a preposterous story. So extreme, sir, one can't take it as truth. One can only laugh. *(Lights rise on The Marquis. He writes on sheets of torn linen, using a stick as a pen, dipping it into his carafe of wine.)*

THE MARQUIS. Here follow the adventures of Monsieur Dolmance, who could not raise his scepter without first submerging it in a vial filled with the tears of maligned virgins. To procure the precious fluid, he first sent his coachmen into the night to kidnap the unsuspecting damsels. A simple line always sufficed: "Mademoiselle, your mother is perilously ill! I must take you to her at once!" Once the maids were sequestered in his dungeon, Dolmance employed many exotic means to harvest their sobs — wrapping their feet with nettles, salting their wounds, and strafing their backs with his cane. Soon, the chalice was filled. Dolmance dunked his harpoon, then lanced each of his wailing captives in turn. *(Lights fade on The Marquis.)*

DR. ROYER-COLLARD. His scribbling is no less potent for its form!

MADELEINE. After reading them, Mama and I, fearful of

33

their discovery, attempted to wash away the words! And so the vats were polluted!

DR. ROYER-COLLARD.   Why would a demure young girl such as yourself, not to mention your aging Mother, indulge in such pornography?

MADELEINE.   It's hard day's wages, sir, slaving away at the behest of madmen. What we've seen in life, it takes a lot to hold our interest.

DR. ROYER-COLLARD.   But why would you want to heap such ghastly fantasies atop an already ghastly existence?

MADELEINE.   We put ourselves in his stories, sir. We play the parts. Poor blind Mama, a countess. Me, a courtesan. We've acted them all, you see, regardless of sex — each atheist, each barbarian. And in our dreams, sir ... it's us doing the killings.

DR. ROYER-COLLARD.   *You?*

MADELEINE.   Revenge our only motive; rage our only Master.

DR. ROYER-COLLARD.   To what end?

MADELEINE.   If we weren't such bad women on the page, Doctor, I'll hazard we couldn't be such good women in life. *(Lights fade on Madeleine.)*

COULMIER.   He is indeed a maniac, and matchless at that!

DR. ROYER-COLLARD.   You assured me that his writing had ceased.

COULMIER.   I hoped it had.

DR. ROYER-COLLARD.   The time has come to adopt more punitive means.

COULMIER.   If only I trusted their efficacy!

DR. ROYER-COLLARD.   When a child pilfers from the candy dish, what do we offer for his reformation? Do we remove temptation altogether, depriving him *and ourselves* of sweetmeats?

COULMIER.   No, sir.

DR. ROYER-COLLARD.   Do we numb him with philosophy? Great diatribes wherein we debate the nature of good and evil?

COULMIER.   I suppose not, sir.

DR. ROYER-COLLARD.   Do we promise him an everlasting afterlife, plucking harps, should he return the bonbon to its

rightful seat? *Or do we toss him over our knee, yank down his breeches, and thrash him with the rod?*
COULMIER.   The latter, unfortunately. And so he learns to fear punishment, rather than to pursue virtue for its own reward.
DR. ROYER-COLLARD.   You're a sentimental man.
COULMIER.   A practical man, sir. Given The Marquis' unusual tastes, a sound thrashing on bare flesh may not qualify as a "deterrent."
DR. ROYER-COLLARD.   I will not be embarrassed a second time.

Scene 8

Coulmier, The Marquis.

THE MARQUIS.   My lilac, my dove!
COULMIER.   I am not here for sport.
THE MARQUIS.   You've come to continue our debate?
COULMIER.   Hardly. From now on, you will sleep on a bare mattress.
THE MARQUIS.   What, and freeze to death?
COULMIER.   And for good measure, we'll seize the curtains, the towels and the rugs.
THE MARQUIS.   My room, stripped bare?
COULMIER.   And nothing but water at every meal.
THE MARQUIS.   No, you can't! Deny me anything but the grape!
COULMIER.   I am sorry. It's decided.
THE MARQUIS.   My circulation — I am not a young man! And my insomnia — alcohol is my only elixir!
COULMIER.   Please. That's quite enough.
THE MARQUIS.   ONE DROP NIGHTLY, THAT'S ALL I ASK! SHOW MERCY, PLEASE!
COULMIER.   Your meat shall be de-boned. You'll have nothing you might fashion as a quill.

THE MARQUIS. *Why this sudden torture?*

COULMIER. I have not been emphatic enough with you, Marquis. Your degrading habits continue, unabated.

THE MARQUIS. It was only for her.

COULMIER. For whom?

THE MARQUIS. The girl. To entice her back to me. Those splendid afternoons when — for a brief, shining moment — she toppled these stone walls, and set me free.

COULMIER. Her visits, too, will be curtailed.

THE MARQUIS. Her gentle sway may be the final lifeline cast to me. Let me seize it, so I might at last be towed into the warm, cerulean waters of a Virtuous Life!

COULMIER. The purplest prose is always the least sincere.

THE MARQUIS. It's a potent aphrodisiac, isn't it, my dumpling?

COULMIER. What's that?

THE MARQUIS. Power over another man.

COULMIER. It pains me to censure you. It is not my nature. I am, as you know, a charitable man.

THE MARQUIS. Most.

COULMIER. You're lucky it falls to me to reprimand you. If it were up to the Doctor, you'd be more than castigated. You'd be flayed alive!

THE MARQUIS. A man after my own heart!

COULMIER. He'd not share your wine, laugh at your vulgarities, and humor you with argument —

THE MARQUIS. You're his sycophant, aren't you? He cracks the whip, and you dance. Don't be shy, Coulmier. Jig for me.

COULMIER. Why, you scornful little weasel —

THE MARQUIS. Follow the steps he's taught you; you'd best not improvise....

COULMIER. The Doctor and I have our differences, but on this point we uniformly agree: *you are a baneful miasma, and you must be purged! (The Marquis begins to dance.)*

THE MARQUIS. Ah-one and a two and a three and a four, ah-one and a two and a three and a four —

COULMIER. Good day, Marquis. *(He turns to leave. The Marquis stops dancing, and hisses:)*

THE MARQUIS. Psst. Plug-tail. My little skin-flute ...
COULMIER. What now?
THE MARQUIS. In conditions of adversity, the artist thrives.

Scene 9

Dr. Royer-Collard, Coulmier, Madeleine, The Marquis.

Madeleine cowers in the office of Dr. Royer-Collard. He slaps a switch across the surface of his desk.

DR. ROYER-COLLARD. If your mother lacks either the means or intelligence to punish you for your foolishness, then perhaps it's my duty to parent you in her stead.
MADELEINE. No, sir! Please, sir!
DR. ROYER-COLLARD. I've no compunction, young lady, about driving my point home with a few, swift strokes of the birch. *(Coulmier enters.)*
MADELEINE. Dear Abbe! You're a man of God, sir. Show me one small drop of His infinite mercy ...
COULMIER. What's this, child? Shivering like a leaf? Surely you've done no wrong.
MADELEINE. He means to whip me senseless!
COULMIER. Is it true, Doctor?
DR. ROYER-COLLARD. It all depends, Abbe, on her cooperation.
MADELEINE. I've such pale, thin skin! I bruise quickly, and in the most repellent hues!
COULMIER. Shh, child. Gather your wits. I'll see that you come to no harm.
MADELEINE. It's true what the lunatics say, Abbe. You are the kinder man.
COULMIER. Pray, Doctor. What's happened here? And why is this poor girl undone?
DR. ROYER-COLLARD. This morning, I sent Valcour to the

37

laundry. I thought — given the recent turn of events — it would be prudent to conduct a search.

COULMIER.   And just what did Valcour find there?

MADELEINE.   A little gift, that's all, meant only for me.

DR. ROYER-COLLARD.   And from whom was this gift bequeathed to you?

MADELEINE.   From himself. The Marquis.

COULMIER.   The Marquis?

MADELEINE.   He pretended to leave some mending for me, outside the door. A souvenir, of sorts.

DR. ROYER-COLLARD.   And what was the nature of this memento?

MADELEINE.   'Twas a chapter! Culled from his latest masterpiece!

COULMIER.   But that's not possible. His cell is barren. No pen, no paper. His linens stripped, his carafe dry. He has nothing to fashion into pages.

DR. ROYER-COLLARD.   That's what you think.

MADELEINE.   Some men aren't mad at all. We only think them so, because their genius so far exceeds our own.

DR. ROYER-COLLARD.   SHOW HIM. *NOW. (Hesitantly, Madeleine produces a shirt, with broad sleeves and a host of ruffles. It's decorated with cursive.)*

COULMIER.   Where in God's name did he procure ink?

MADELEINE.   Nowhere. He pricked the tips of his fingers with a carving knife. His latest fancies — they're scripted in blood.

COULMIER.   Dear God, preserve us.

DR. ROYER-COLLARD.   I decided to confront The Marquis myself. When I hoisted open the gates of the South Wing, there he was, strolling about the corridor. His blouse and breeches were covered in script. He'd turned his very wardrobe into text! The idiot Giton was reading his leggings, while the hysteric Michete perused his vest. *(Lights rise on The Marquis. His clothes are awash with words.)*

THE MARQUIS.   My newest book begins at my right cuff, continues across my back, and completes itself at the base of my left shoe.

COULMIER. Never was a wardrobe more vulgar in design!

THE MARQUIS. Monsieur Bouloir was a man whose sexual appetites might discreetly be described as "post-mortem." A habitué of cemeteries, his proudest conquest was that of a maid six decades his senior, deceased a dozen years. The vigor with which he frigged caused her bones to dislodge. Still he granted her the highest compliment he accorded any woman: *"WELL WORTH THE DIG!."*

COULMIER. NOOOOOOOO!

Scene 10

Coulmier, The Marquis.

COULMIER. You! YOU! Such brazen defiance! Flouncing about like some demented peacock!

THE MARQUIS. Don't tell me. You've come to read my trousers. You'll note the longest sentence trails down the inseam.

COULMIER. How could you! Parading your decadence before the helpless and the sick!

THE MARQUIS. Piffle!

COULMIER. Your stories so aroused poor Michete, we've had to tie him to his bedposts.

THE MARQUIS. Lucky Michete. You tell him that there are some very reputable individuals, notable in French society, who pay good money to be tied to their bedposts.

COULMIER. What am I to do with you, Marquis? The more I forbid, the more you are provoked.

THE MARQUIS. My darling Coulmier. Here, in my dank quarters, I've had ample time to ruminate on our little tussle. And I've come to a conclusion you'll no doubt find deliriously satisfying.

COULMIER. I'm holding my breath.

THE MARQUIS. Headstrong though I may be, I could be

convinced to abandon my writing. Quite voluntarily.

COULMIER.   And what in God's name would that require?
A thousand livres?

THE MARQUIS.   Tsk, tsk, tsk. Much cheaper.

COULMIER.   Your room, restored to its luster.

THE MARQUIS.   Much simpler.

COULMIER.   Your freedom.

THE MARQUIS.   I wouldn't dream of it.

COULMIER.   What then?

THE MARQUIS.   A night, sugar-plum, spent with the part-
ner of my choice.

COULMIER.   Aha! I should've known!

THE MARQUIS.   A lover who will set all pride aside, and
allow me to plumb with my lubricious engine the twin cheeks
of delight.

COULMIER.   Write countless unseemly tomes, Marquis. I will
not pimp poor Madeleine!

THE MARQUIS.   I wasn't talking about Madeleine.

COULMIER.   Then who?

THE MARQUIS.   *You, my precious. (Coulmier turns a fiery red.
He bellows:)*

COULMIER.   OFF WITH YOUR CLOTHES!

THE MARQUIS.   Coulmier, you rascal!

COULMIER.   OFF, I SAY!

THE MARQUIS.   Has my proposal so enflamed you?

COULMIER.   I DO NOT MEAN TO *FLIRT,* MARQUIS!

THE MARQUIS.   Oh but you must, my pumpkin! Sex without flirtation is merely rape!

COULMIER.   Damn you, Marquis! You are beyond villainy!
You are the Devil! NOW STRIP! *(The Marquis begins to undress.)*

THE MARQUIS.   My doublet?

COULMIER.   Off!

THE MARQUIS.   My collar?

COULMIER.   Off!

THE MARQUIS.   My shoes; they're naught but punctuation ...

COULMIER.   Off!

THE MARQUIS.   My chintz, my lace, my gabardine?

COULMIER.   Off, off, off!

THE MARQUIS.   Permit me to retain my gauzy underpinnings!

COULMIER.   Every stitch!

THE MARQUIS.   WON'T YOU JOIN ME, PONY-BOY?

COULMIER.   You shall no longer leave your cell, understood? You'll lay your eyes on none but me from now on!

THE MARQUIS.   Such abuse!

COULMIER.   You will not render me a fool!

THE MARQUIS.   I need not render you a fool!

COULMIER.   I have been far too lax with you, Monsieur! Now you shall live as our Father intended — less like a man, and more like the beast you are! Naked, in a hollow pit!

THE MARQUIS.   As lived the noble savages of Lescaux, where even today their glorious paintings remain, undimmed by time!

COULMIER.   HOW DARE YOU DEFEND YOURSELF IN ART'S NAME! HOW DARE YOU RANK YOURSELF WITH THE LIKES OF VOLTAIRE, PASCAL AND RACINE! THEIR QUILLS ARE GUIDED BY THE HAND OF GOD, WHILE YOUR EVERY UTTERANCE IS MALIGNANCY UNMASKED! *(The Marquis has stripped himself bare, save for his hair.)* YOUR WIG! REMOVE YOUR WIG! *(The Marquis does.)*

THE MARQUIS.   How prudent you are, Abbe. I'd planned to curl my locks in the shape of letters, and write a Paean to Buggery that would trail down my backside, and bob at my ass.

COULMIER.   You will not spread your insidious gospel, where tyranny is the norm, and goodness the last refuge of the weak! Where indifferent Nature rails, untempered by the presence of a God! Where art's magnitude is the breadth of its depravity! NO!

THE MARQUIS.   No?

COULMIER.   YOU WILL NOT EVEN WRITE YOUR OWN IGNOMINIOUS NAME!

THE MARQUIS.   Tsk, tsk, tsk. *Are your convictions so fragile that mine cannot stand in opposition to them? Is your God so illusory that the presence of my Devil reveals His insufficiency?* Oh, for shame!

41

COULMIER.   May you spend eternity in the company of your beloved Anti-Christ, turning on his spit! *(He makes for the door.)*
THE MARQUIS.   My suckling ... my lip leech ...
COULMIER.   WHAT?
THE MARQUIS.   My truest quill lies betwixt my thighs. When it fills with ink and rises to the fore.... Oh, the wondrous books it will write!

Scene 11

The Marquis, Madeleine.

THE MARQUIS.   Madeleine!
MADELEINE.   Marquis! Your every inch, exposed!
THE MARQUIS.   This is how your employer chooses to keep me. Like a Roman sculpture, undraped!
MADELEINE.   I'm ashamed to look!
THE MARQUIS.   Surely you've seen a man naked?
MADELEINE.   No, sir. It's only been described to me, in your books.
THE MARQUIS.   Then you've had a most painstaking teacher. I've devoted many a page to the male form. Its rippling hillsides, its undulating prairies, and its crested mount ...
MADELEINE.   Is your body, then, somewhat ... representative?
THE MARQUIS.   For a man my age, and victim of my calumnies.
MADELEINE.   I must say, sir, in your novels, you stoke the most unrealistic expectations. *(The Marquis crosses his legs.)*
THE MARQUIS.   You're far crueler than I, my sweet.
MADELEINE.   I risk terrible danger, coming to see you this way.
THE MARQUIS.   Your life, and your mother's besides.
MADELEINE.   It was guilt which ushered me here, stronger than any commandment. How you must hate me.

THE MARQUIS.   Never!

MADELEINE.   But surely you know it's I who betrayed you to Dr. Royer-Collard. I gave him your soiled bed sheets, and your shirt besides ...

THE MARQUIS.   And I love you the more for it.

MADELEINE.   How can that be?

THE MARQUIS.   I may be a scamp, a chancre and a blight, my blessed Madeleine, but I am not a hypocrite! Don't you see, that by informing against me, you affirm my principles?

MADELEINE.   I'm afraid I don't understand.

THE MARQUIS.   You were willing to sacrifice me on the block to achieve your own gain ...

MADELEINE.   Hence, my sorrow!

THE MARQUIS.   In the animal kingdom, does the tiger spare his sister the doe? Not when he's hungry! That, Madeleine, is natural order! A carefully orchestrated cycle of consumption which we all too often violate with our false codes of law and morality. But you! You rose above such petty constructs, and fed yourself upon my very carcass.

MADELEINE.   And so I am endeared to you?

THE MARQUIS.   I stand before you, not in rage, but awe.

MADELEINE.   You're a queer one, all right.

THE MARQUIS.   Can you smuggle a paper and quill to me?

MADELEINE.   If only! Mother and I, we're weak with boredom, our evenings spent in silence. For a while, I smuggled home old newspapers from the scullery, and read their accounts of the Terror. She found those too barbaric, and pined for your stories instead.

THE MARQUIS.   Never fear, my angel. I have a plan.

MADELEINE.   Let me be its agent, I beg you, as penance for my wrongs against you!

THE MARQUIS.   Take note, beloved, of this chink in the stone. I'll whisper a new tale to my neighbor, the lunatic Cleante. He'll in turn whisper it to his neighbor, Dauphin. Dauphin will impart the tale to the retard Franval, and he will impart it likewise to the noisome Bouchon —

MADELEINE.   Whose cell lies next to the linen cabinet!

THE MARQUIS.   Precisely!

MADELEINE.   And there, armed with a quill of my own, I'll receive your story through the wall, and commit it to paper!

THE MARQUIS.   Voilà!

MADELEINE.   Oh, Marquis! How ingenious you are!

THE MARQUIS.   Imagine! My scandalous stories, whipping through the halls of this mausoleum, like some mysterious breeze! A string of tongues, all wagging in service of my prose.

MADELEINE.   But with men whose minds are so weak, will your art survive such a journey?

THE MARQUIS.   My heinous vision, filtered through the minds of the insane. Who knows? They might improve it!

MADELEINE.   I'll practice my hand, Marquis, and do your words justice.

THE MARQUIS.   You can take them home to Mother, and on to my publisher besides!

MADELEINE.   Only one thing troubles me …

THE MARQUIS.   Fear of discovery?

MADELEINE.   No. Fear of the inmate Bouchon, the agent closest to me in the line.

THE MARQUIS.   Why him, more than any other?

MADELEINE.   He holds a torch for me. Once, when I was darning his stockings, he pressed me hard against the wall, and his stinking breath caused my eyes to run. It was the Abbe de Coulmier who saved me.

THE MARQUIS.   What of it?

MADELEINE.   Well, sir, given the potency of your stories, and the fragility of his brain … it might cause a combustion; that's all.

THE MARQUIS.   What are we to do, dearest? Shuffle the patients in their cells? That's not within our power. Now, accept the danger, or withdraw.

MADELEINE.   I accept.

THE MARQUIS.   Madeleine…?

MADELEINE.   Yes, Marquis?

THE MARQUIS.   A kiss per page. The price holds.

MADELEINE.   But how can I? We're forbidden to meet.

THE MARQUIS.   Which is why this time, my pussy-willow, I must request payment in advance.

MADELEINE.   You're a caution, you are!

THE MARQUIS.   Quickly, before we are discovered! *(They consume one another with kisses.)*

Scene 12

The Marquis, A Lunatic, The Voices of the Insane.

A crack of thunder. Rain begins to pelt the stone walls of Charenton.

Alone, The Marquis whispers into a crack in the wall.

THE MARQUIS.   Psst ... Cleante? Are you there? *(A voice answers.)*

A LUNATIC.   Marquis? Is that you?

THE MARQUIS.   Who else would it be?

A LUNATIC.   I've the most wonderful news, Marquis! I'm no longer a man! This morning, I awoke a bird!

THE MARQUIS.   *Quiet!*

A LUNATIC.   Tonight, I'll fly through the bars of my cell to freedom!

THE MARQUIS.   Listen to what I say, and report it post-haste to your neighbor Dauphin.

A LUNATIC.   I've huge, flapping wings, and a beak for scavenging! And I can warble, too! *(The Lunatic begins to trill.)*

THE MARQUIS.   CLEANTE!

A LUNATIC.   Eh?

THE MARQUIS.   I've news for you too, pigeon. This morning I awoke a cat.

A LUNATIC.   A cat, Count?

THE MARQUIS.   *(Dryly.)* Meow.

A LUNATIC.   No! I implore you! Anything but that!

THE MARQUIS.   If you don't do what I tell you, I'll claw through this wall, and eat you alive. I'll sink my little fangs into your drumsticks, and suck the marrow straight out of your bones.

A LUNATIC.   At your service, Count!

THE MARQUIS.   And so we begin. Our story concerns the young heroine Fanchon, a harlot in a harem reputed to be the most varied in all Europe: there, you could plow a Prussian princess, sodomize twins, or tickle the loins of a Hungarian Dwarf. *(Down the corridor, faintly, we hear other voices pick up the tale.)*

THE VOICES OF THE INSANE.   Tickle the loins of a Hungarian Dwarf ... tickle the loins ... the loins ... the loins ... the loins ...

THE MARQUIS.   One day Fanchon was visited by a certain Monsieur De Curval, an accomplished surgeon, and an even more renowned Libertine. He had been barred from many of the city's finer brothels, so lethal were his exploits.

THE VOICES OF THE INSANE.   So lethal were his exploits ... so lethal ... so lethal ... lethal ...

THE MARQUIS.   Once they were secluded in her bedchamber, he bade Fanchon strip, and strip she did, with the speed of one unaccustomed to clothing's confinement. As she stood naked before him, he ran his fingers across her skin, pulling apart folds of flesh, inspecting follicles.

THE VOICES OF THE INSANE.   Pulling apart folds of flesh ... folds of flesh ... flesh ... flesh ...

THE MARQUIS.   "What shall I ready, Monsieur?" asked Fanchon. "My mouth, my rounded ass or my Venus mound, my succulent oyster?"

THE VOICES OF THE INSANE.   My Venus mound, my succulent oyster ... succulent oyster ... oyster ... oyster ...

THE MARQUIS.   "None!" cried Monsieur de Curval, brandishing a scalpel he had hidden in his breast. "With my blade, I'll create new orifices, where there were none before! Once hewn, I can thrust my turgid member into regions unsullied by your previous suitors!"

THE VOICES OF THE INSANE.   Unsullied suitors ... suitors ... suitors ... suitors ...

THE MARQUIS.   With that, Fanchon expelled a scream so

extravagantly pitched that the Libertine was obliged to tear out her tongue, cauterizing the wound with a poker from the fire. Next, he splayed her body across the mattress, and with the edge of his knife — *(From off, in the distance, a sudden scream. It slices through the air, and echoes down the corridor. The Marquis stops short. His face goes white. He recognizes the howling voice. A bolt of lightning, as powerful as the zap that martyred poor Justine. We see — for a single, blistering moment — the body of Madeleine. She's been hoisted from a rafter in the laundry room, and spins, wildly. Her body is a study in carnage. The face of The Marquis contorts in pain. A sudden lurch, and he collapses on the floor, his body wracked by sobs. Blackness. The blowing of the wind. The curtain falls.)*

END OF ACT ONE

ACT TWO

Scene 1

Renée Pélagie, Dr. Royer-Collard.

RENÉE PÉLAGIE.   'Twas a night fraught with terror! I'll never again tremble at tales of the Last Judgment, or wince at depictions of the Tortures of the Damned. For Hell has indeed been visited upon the earth, and it happened right here at the Charenton Asylum.

DR. ROYER-COLLARD.   You over-state our misadventure, Madame.

RENÉE PÉLAGIE.   Do I? Or are you — perhaps — reluctant to confront the facts?

DR. ROYER-COLLARD.   It was a skirmish; nothing more.

RENÉE PÉLAGIE.   Your charge here is to bring order to an unruly hospital. And instead — *on your watch* — the patients revolt, setting their cots ablaze, and hurling furniture from their cells. I myself saw a porcelain commode flung from the parapet! And what were the guards doing, I ask you? Stifling the fray? Ha! *They were running for their very lives!*

DR. ROYER-COLLARD.   I hasten to assure you — just as I assured the Ministry and the Police Inspector before you — that harmony within our walls has been restored.

RENÉE PÉLAGIE.   All of Saint-Maurice turned out for the fracas. *Your riot, sir, was the most scrupulously attended social affair since Madame Rougemont's summer cotillion!* The Baron De Cordier stood peering through the iron gates, in hopes of catching a glimpse of the furor within. Madame Bougival bid her coachmen stop, and scrambled for her telescope. And what did they see? Oh, Doctor, sights so depraved and bizarre, that I can barely find the words to describe them!

DR. ROYER-COLLARD.   I have a sinking feeling you'll rise

to the occasion.

RENÉE PÉLAGIE. Crazed women hiking their skirts to the heavens, and pawing at their own femininity! Men with vacant eyes and frothy mouths, their trousers about their ankles, swinging their attributes like pendulums! And who, Sir, was the conductor of this demonic orchestra? The ring-master of this Luciferian circus? WHO? *MY HUSBAND, OF COURSE!*

DR. ROYER-COLLARD. It seems he treated the patients to ... an oral recitation. They were regrettably ... *over-stimulated* ... by its contents.

RENÉE PÉLAGIE. "Over-stimulated," Doctor? They were hanging out the windows, polluting themselves! Charenton became a bawdy house! A brothel for the feeble-minded! *A cat-house for the loons! (She collapses into a chair, fanning herself wildly.)* Ah! Ah! He's done it. The Marquis has — at long last — broken my heart. I can feel it in my breast, cleft in twain. I must have smelling salts! A glass of water! Absinthe! *Anything, Doctor, quickly! (Dr. Royer-Collard hands Renée Pélagie a small snuff-box. She imbibes.)*

DR. ROYER-COLLARD. Sparingly, Madame. You'll singe your membranes.

RENÉE PÉLAGIE. His little fable traveled far. One of your wards told the cook; the cook told his wife; she told the cobbler; and so on and so on, ad infinitum! Even now, the story is lumbering toward Paris, like some carnivorous, hump-backed beast. Who knows what lascivious behavior it leaves in its wake?

DR. ROYER-COLLARD. My chief worry is not for Charenton or for France, but for you. I know the ridicule you have borne on your husband's behalf.

RENÉE PÉLAGIE. Don't patronize me, Doctor. I hold you in no less contempt than my husband.

DR. ROYER-COLLARD. Me? But why?

RENÉE PÉLAGIE. Last night's episode was completely avoidable. If only you'd remained true to our contract.

DR. ROYER-COLLARD. I beg your pardon?

RENÉE PÉLAGIE. Was it your immediate intention to swindle me? Or did the plot dawn on you slowly, over time, like a gathering thundercloud?

DR. ROYER-COLLARD. I'm afraid I don't follow.

RENÉE PÉLAGIE. At your insistence, sir, I provided the necessary funds for a host of refurbishments. *(She pulls out a list, and reads:)* Thirty-three brass hospital beds, each fitted with restraints, twelve branding irons, a bed of nails, a set of steel-tipped martinets, and — finally — a St. Andrew's Cross. And have you purchased even a single item? NO!

DR. ROYER-COLLARD. I can say, with the utmost sincerity, that every franc you've given me has been put to sterling use.

RENÉE PÉLAGIE. Perhaps I have a suspicious mind, Doctor. But that fortress you're constructing on the southern edge of town ...

DR. ROYER-COLLARD. What of it?

RENÉE PÉLAGIE. Well. People talk. Mirrors made from Venetian glass. Walls covered in Chinese silk. A balustrade pilfered from a Russian palace ...

DR. ROYER-COLLARD. Surely you recognize that my success in these halls is contingent upon my comfort. And that my *comfort*, in turn, depends on my *surroundings*. Every stone laid, each ounce of mortar spread, each molded crest abutting each window frame, hastens your husband's recovery!

RENÉE PÉLAGIE. You must admit it's odd. Your poor hospital can't even afford a whipping post. And all the while, you sit at home, sipping fumé blanc on a Grecian divan ...

DR. ROYER-COLLARD. I am appalled, Madame, to see a woman of your standing stoop to crass innuendo.

RENÉE PÉLAGIE. Either the Ministry rewards you with a king's ransom, or *someone has his fingers in my till!*

DR. ROYER-COLLARD. You would enter my office, sally up to my desk, and accuse me of common thievery?

RENÉE PÉLAGIE. I wouldn't call it "common," sir. Impudent. Shameless. Bald. But never "common!"

DR. ROYER-COLLARD. This room has played host to the most caustic minds. Still, I've never been so insulted.

RENÉE PÉLAGIE. I urge you to take concrete action to silence my husband, or expect a second visit from my lawyer of a far graver nature than the first. *(She barrels for the door, then turns with a flourish:)* Good day, sir!

Scene 2

Dr. Royer-Collard, Coulmier, The Marquis.

COULMIER.   The fire in the belfry has been doused. We quieted the horses in the stables. And the patients have all been firmly strapped back into their beds. Call me a fool, but I hope that you've summoned me this morning to relay *good* news.

DR. ROYER-COLLARD.   You're a fool.

COULMIER.   Touché.

DR. ROYER-COLLARD.   Your failure has cost an innocent life.

COULMIER.   I beg your pardon?

DR. ROYER-COLLARD.   The seamstress, Madeleine Leclerc.

COULMIER.   Madeleine ... dead?

DR. ROYER-COLLARD.   Last night, in the melee, the inmate Bouchon burst the confines of his cell and tortured the poor child until she expired.

COULMIER.   *What?*

DR. ROYER-COLLARD.   She was discovered this morning, splayed like a newly hung carcass, in the laundry. Bouchon was so favorably impressed by The Marquis' tale that he chose to re-enact it. Lovingly, and with admirable fidelity to the author. Each laceration. Each swathe of the blade.

COULMIER.   Poor Madeleine! To spend her last hours at the mercy of that ham-fisted *brute*, that *ogre* ...

DR. ROYER-COLLARD.   We mustn't blame Bouchon. If he possessed restraint ... conscience ... morality ... he'd have no need of us, would he? No, the fault lies elsewhere, I'm afraid.

COULMIER.   Of course.

DR. ROYER-COLLARD.   It is our duty, is it not, to protect malleable minds from pernicious influence?

COULMIER.   I suppose it is.

DR. ROYER-COLLARD.   To admonish the individual, when

his habits impinge upon the safety of the whole?

COULMIER. Yes, Doctor.

DR. ROYER-COLLARD. And when we falter at this charge?

COULMIER. Bedlam, sir. And death.

DR. ROYER-COLLARD. If I seem severe to you ... tyranni-cal, even ... it's because we owe our dependents nothing less. We must provide for them what they cannot muster for them-selves. *Dominion over the beast within.*

COULMIER. If you'll pardon me, Doctor, it was an endless night.

DR. ROYER-COLLARD. How many other tragedies must be-fall Charenton before you embrace your duty here?

COULMIER. My head has yet to touch a pillow, my lips to taste a meal —

DR. ROYER-COLLARD. Would that you had seen the girl's mother. Her face stained with tears, her eyes glazed, uncom-prehending. I thank God, because of her blindness, she was spared the sight of her daughter's riddled corpse.

COULMIER. I'll make reparation to the family.

DR. ROYER-COLLARD. There's another matter that you'd better address first.

COULMIER. Of course.

DR. ROYER-COLLARD. Might I suggest a stroll down the West Wing. Take a look at the operating theater. You'll find everything you need there.

COULMIER. That room's been locked for twenty years.

DR. ROYER-COLLARD. The douche chair, the brazier slab, the fustigator, the Procrustean bed, and the abdominal wagon. They're all at your disposal.

COULMIER. It sounds less like a hospital, Doctor, and more akin to a chamber of horrors.

DR. ROYER-COLLARD. How perceptive, Abbe.

COULMIER. Knowing my disposition toward such cruel mea-sures ... *(Dr. Royer-Collard glares.)* Must you.... Mustn't we.... Must I.... I must ... *(Dr. Royer-Collard clears his throat.)* I must have the key, sir. I've long since misplaced mine. *(Dr. Royer-Collard hands Coulmier the key.)*

DR. ROYER-COLLARD. When you lay your head upon the

pillow tonight, beg God's forgiveness for the death of poor Madeleine. You shan't have mine.

Scene 3

Coulmier, The Marquis.

THE MARQUIS.   Suppose one of your precious wards had attempted to walk on water, and drowned. Would you condemn the Bible? I think not!

COULMIER.   Would that he had only injured himself, and not another.

THE MARQUIS.   Am I to be held responsible for the actions of every half-wit here?

COULMIER.   The man who loads the cannon and the man who fires it are both culpable, Marquis.

THE MARQUIS.   It was fiction! It was not intended as "How-to!" Castigate Bouchon, not me.

COULMIER.   Bouchon is not a man; he's an overgrown child.

THE MARQUIS.   So I am to tailor my writing for imbeciles?

COULMIER.   You weren't to be writing at all!

THE MARQUIS.   A writer cannot answer for his audience!

COULMIER.   He must, when he incites it to crime!

THE MARQUIS.   The experience of art — MY LITTLE BULL'S PIZZLE — is a *collaborative affair.* The author provides the stimuli; the reader his response. All I can control is the art itself; my subject, culled from life, and told with an eye toward truth, or — at least — truth as life has taught me to perceive it. And you must concede, SWEETUMS, that life has taught me some very scabrous tidbits indeed! And so I record them! Dutifully! As any writer should! BUT — the *response* to my work. Well, POODLE, that's a fickle thing indeed. It may be prompted by the reader's race! His sex! His politics! The potency of the beer he drank with dinner! The angle of his bed! *Even the last time he diddled his wife!* In short, variables well

53

beyond the scope of the artist. What am I to do, POLICE MY READERS AS YOU POLICE ME? HA!

COULMIER. You wish to know the sum impact of your work upon the public, Marquis?

THE MARQUIS. Pray, tell?

COULMIER. INNOCENT PEOPLE DIE.

THE MARQUIS. So many authors are denied the gratification of a concrete response to their toiling. I am blessed, am I not?

COULMIER. I labored under the misconception that you felt something for the young girl. That in some dark, crusted, corroded corner of your heart, she touched you.

THE MARQUIS. She was flirtatious, to me and to others.

COULMIER. Don't you dare start on this course.

THE MARQUIS. Her breasts heaving under poplin. Her ass, like two melons, bobbling at the bottom of a sack ...

COULMIER. You'll do yourself no credit by pursuing this line ...

THE MARQUIS. Bouchon has done us all a favor, nipping temptation in the bud.

COULMIER. It is no secret, Marquis, that you loved her.

THE MARQUIS. Ha!

COULMIER. It was many a time you tore a hole in your topcoat, only to secure her services!

THE MARQUIS. Rubbish!

COULMIER. You bartered pages for a single kiss.

THE MARQUIS. Who told you this?

COULMIER. You doted on her!

THE MARQUIS. Was it she?

COULMIER. You worshipped her!

THE MARQUIS. Flattering herself, I suppose!

COULMIER. *You were her slave!*

THE MARQUIS. I WANTED TO FUCK HER, THAT'S ALL!

COULMIER. AND DID YOU?

THE MARQUIS. IT IS NOT YOUR PROVINCE TO ASK!

COULMIER. You're no stranger to rape, Marquis! And yet with her, you cooed. You courted. You begged.

THE MARQUIS. Go to hell!

COULMIER. WHY WAS IT YOU NEVER TOOK HER BY FORCE?

THE MARQUIS. WHO IS TO SAY I DID NOT?

COULMIER. Was it impotence?

THE MARQUIS. NEVER!

COULMIER. Was it polite deference?

THE MARQUIS. The only witness is Madeleine herself, and her lips — and her body — are sealed.

COULMIER. Was it HUMANE REGARD? WAS IT — GASP! — LOVE???? *(The Marquis chokes on Coulmier's last word.)*

THE MARQUIS. *I FUCKED HER A THOUSAND TIMES! WITH PNEUMATIC FORCE!*

COULMIER. We inspected the body, Marquis. She died intact. *(A stunned pause. The Marquis cracks — a tiny cry at first, which erupts into genuine sobbing. Finally, he speaks. His voice is barely a whisper:)*

THE MARQUIS. You will see she receives a proper burial. In the churchyard. At my expense. I implore you … do not inter her sweet body in the same ground as the madmen and the devils who inhabit this accursed place. *(A pause.)*

COULMIER. Your terrible secret, revealed. You are a man after all. *(The Marquis looks at Coulmier a moment. Suddenly — sharply — he spits at him. Coulmier wipes away the indignity.)* All that remains now is your punishment.

THE MARQUIS. Your lily mind cannot compete with mine in this department.

COULMIER. For that I'm grateful.

THE MARQUIS. What "frightful torture" have you devised, kitten?

COULMIER. I have knelt in the chapel and consorted with God. I have asked him if I am justified in my measures. And he has assured me that I am.

THE MARQUIS. What will it be, my little dictator?

COULMIER. Blood has been spilled, and regrettably, I must spill more to stem its ruby tide.

THE MARQUIS. The logic of a true warrior. Congratulations.

COULMIER. Don't deride me, murderer.

THE MARQUIS. Well? Don't keep me in suspense. Fifty

lashes? A night on the rack?

COULMIER. Tonight, you'll be ... ah ... you will be ... visited by the ...

THE MARQUIS. You haven't the stomach for this, have you?

COULMIER. I have ... authorized ... the procedure myself ...

THE MARQUIS. You haven't the balls.

COULMIER. It is our sad duty, Marquis, to ... to ...

THE MARQUIS. Weakling! Runt! Crab louse!

COULMIER. Oh, dear merciful God ...

THE MARQUIS. Up in your office, buoyed by your cronies, it was easy to devise my undoing, wasn't it? *Wasn't it?* A regular parlor game. Each of you, chirping, like giddy magpies. "Solitary confinement! Perhaps we'll dock his dessert. Maybe a good spanking. Ouch!" But now, face-to-face with your victim, you're turning soft. After all, I'm not some stranger. I'm your *friend*, The Marquis. *(He extends his hand to Coulmier.)* I dare you. Stab my flesh. Which one of us will bleed? *(Coulmier stares at him a moment, and takes a few paces toward the door.)* Ha! I knew it.

COULMIER. Tonight, you'll be visited by the surgeon. He'll cut out your tongue. *(A pause. Finally:)*

THE MARQUIS. Then surely you'll grant me a final word.

COULMIER. Of course.

THE MARQUIS. I didn't forge the mind of man. Your precious God did that. Cramming it full of rancor and bloodlust. Like Zeus, thrusting all those winged demons, into the tiny confines of Pandora's box. Don't hate me just because I turn the key, and let them loose. "Fly, my darlings, fly! All the way to heaven, till you burst the clouds, and blacken the sun!"

COULMIER. I don't hate you, Marquis. More's the pity. *(He stands, fretful and spent. He swivels to go. Again, The Marquis coos after him.)*

THE MARQUIS. Abbe de Coulmier.

COULMIER. What now? *(The Marquis sticks out his tongue, and makes a clipping gesture.)*

THE MARQUIS. Snip, snip, snip. *(He smiles.)* Would that I were so easily silenced.

Scene 4

Dr. Royer-Collard, Monsieur Prouix, Madame Royer-Collard.

Dr. Royer-Collard sits in his office. He opens a letter from Monsieur Prouix, and begins to read it.

Lights rise on Monsieur Prouix, wearing a loose dressing gown. He sits at a small writing desk, and composes a note.

MONSIEUR PROUIX.   "Most Esteemed Dr. Royer-Collard, At long last, your Chateau is complete. You'll find everything in its assigned place: the chintz draperies, the English bell pulls, even the ivory doorstops. Only one detail is missing ..." *(He emits a series of short, staccato moans, followed by a long sigh. Madame Royer-Collard crawls out from beneath the desk, wearing a corset and pantaloons. She repairs her lipstick.) "Your wife." (He leans down and kisses her hungrily. Madame Royer-Collard cracks a small riding crop in the air.)*
MADAME ROYER-COLLARD.   You obsequious men. Underneath all that scraping and bowing, you're such wolves.
MONSIEUR PROUIX.   "It would seem that — no matter how splendid her surroundings — she cannot resist the urge to cuckold her husband."
MADAME ROYER-COLLARD.   Tell him I'm no fool! A prison's still a prison, with or without wainscoting and Baccarat chandeliers!
MONSIEUR PROUIX.   "And so, I have pirated Marguerite away to a safe haven ..."
MADAME ROYER-COLLARD.   Ooh, ooh, ooh! Tell him — if he uncovers our whereabouts —
MONSIEUR PROUIX.   Yes?
MADAME ROYER-COLLARD.   — you'll slit your wrist with a razor! And I'll plunge a hatpin through my heart!
MONSIEUR PROUIX.   You'd do that, rather than forsake our love?

MADAME ROYER-COLLARD.   No. But tell him I would. (*A pause. Monsieur Prouix frowns.*)
MONSIEUR PROUIX.   I worry, Marguerite, that you don't really love me at all, but merely mean to use me to your own convenient ends, as a vehicle to escape your husband's tyranny.
MADAME ROYER-COLLARD.   You're brighter than you look. Now write. (*Monsieur Prouix shrugs, and obediently writes:*)
MONSIEUR PROUIX.   "A ... hatpin ... through ... my heart ..."
MADAME ROYER-COLLARD.   Sign it quickly. Then carry me upstairs, so you can ravish me again! *On linens for which he so dearly paid!*
MONSIEUR PROUIX.   Yes, Marguerite, yes!
MADAME ROYER-COLLARD.   We'll stain the bedding. We'll dampen the chamois, and leave puddles of love all over the coverlet!
MONSIEUR PROUIX.   On the satin twill ... then, I beg you, on the teakwood floor of the salon ... and please, oh, please ... as a crowning gesture ... *on the ocelot rug in the foyer!* (*As if in answer, Madame Royer-Collard yowls like a cat. Monsieur Prouix signs:*) "Sincerely, Jean-Pierre Prouix." (*Madame Royer-Collard takes the pen from his hand, and adds an epithet:*)
MADAME ROYER-COLLARD.   "*The ... Architect ... of Your ... Unhappy ... Fate!*" (*Monsieur Prouix smiles. He breaks into a laugh; Madame Royer-Collard chimes in. The lights on the couple fade. Dr. Royer-Collard sits, stalwart. He begins to tremble. Slowly, deliberately, he tears the letter into tiny shreds. Blackout.*)

Scene 5

Dr. Royer-Collard, Coulmier, The Marquis.

COULMIER.   The surgeon completed his grim task just as the sun was about to rise. So violent were The Marquis' protestations, that he prolonged his own pain. I have, as you requested, proof of our success. (*Coulmier places a small tin box on Dr. Royer-Collard's desk.)* His tongue, Doctor. So long and serpentine I had to roll it 'round a dowel. Now our grisly business is concluded. We'll never again have to wield the scalpel against The Marquis, or any ward.

DR. ROYER-COLLARD. You are aware, are you not, that even the patients are laughing behind your back?

COULMIER. What?

DR. ROYER-COLLARD. How can they look to you as their Savior, when you inspire ridicule in lieu of respect?

COULMIER. Doctor Royer-Collard, I have fulfilled my duties and beyond. I stood, sir, at the surgeon's side, holding The Marquis fast to his chair, my knees weak and my head swimming, all in the service of Charenton. Now, I refuse to be further baited or debased.

DR. ROYER-COLLARD. Do you know the condition of his room, Abbe?

COULMIER. His room?

DR. ROYER-COLLARD. Words!

COULMIER. Words?

DR. ROYER-COLLARD. Everywhere, words! On the ceiling. Written on the floor. Etched on the walls. A phantasmagoria of words.

COULMIER. No. No. No, no, no, no ...

DR. ROYER-COLLARD. All in his unmistakable script!

COULMIER. But *how?*

DR. ROYER-COLLARD. He spat into his own excrement, and formed a kind of paint.

COULMIER. No, dear God, please ...

DR. ROYER-COLLARD. Finally, a medium worthy of his art. With his fingers, like a child, he decorated the room with language.

COULMIER. Has he no shred of decency?

DR. ROYER-COLLARD. I mustered the patience to follow its scrawl, and found this dense verbiage contained a story.

COULMIER. So the stench of this tale is twofold ...

DR. ROYER-COLLARD. It plunges so deep into the acrid chambers of man's aching heart, that even the angels are left to weep, and the saints to gasp for air. *(Coulmier is sobbing, at*

his wit's end.)
COULMIER.   Don't make me hear it! I beg you! *(Lights rise on The Marquis. He sits, impassive, his lips sewn together. All around him, covering every inch of wall-space, language. Oozing out of each crack, each crevice. Dripping from the ceiling. Lining the floor. We hear his voice.)*
THE VOICE OF THE MARQUIS.   And now — at last — an innocuous tale, sans all perversion, designed to appease my Puritanical captors.
DR. ROYER-COLLARD.   A hollow promise, offered so the story's final twist will shock us all the more.
THE VOICE OF THE MARQUIS.   Monsieur LaFarge was hopelessly smitten by a pretty young maid named Marie Duplaix. He'd long sought her hand in marriage. But each time he proposed, she refused. In hopes of winning her love, Monsieur LaFarge employed the services of a famous Tailor. "You must design a wedding gown," he told the Tailor, "Of such sumptuousness and splendor, that — for the privilege of wearing it — Marie will become my bride." The Tailor bid Marie choose from a host of fabrics. "Kind sir," she cried, "I wish to try them all!" Finally, she alighted on a royal velvet, more costly than a Peau de Soie or Belgian lace. The Tailor drove his needle through the soft fabric, in and out, in and out, in and out, in and out until the dress was done. Marie slipped it on before the glass. The gorgeous gown softened her brittle heart, and so she consented to wed. *(There is a pause. Coulmier is waiting for the voice of The Marquis to continue.)*
COULMIER.   That's it? That's all? *(The Marquis breaks into a hideous smile, through his stitches.)*
THE VOICE OF THE MARQUIS.   Voilà. Happily Ever After. The End. *(Lights fade on The Marquis.)*
COULMIER.   But there's no debauch. No nefarious carousal….
DR. ROYER-COLLARD.   Don't you see? He's trumped us! *He's masked his obscenity with metaphor!*
COULMIER.   He has?
DR. ROYER-COLLARD.   Monsieur LaFarge wants to secure the heart of a winsome young thing. So what does he do? *He*

unwittingly hires his own rival!
COULMIER. He does?
DR. ROYER-COLLARD. Of course! The Tailor!
COULMIER. The Tailor?
DR. ROYER-COLLARD. I can almost see the two of them.
Marie, all dewy and pink in her crinolines. The Tailor, measuring tape in hand, pulling it taut across her heaving breasts ...
COULMIER. Does The Marquis provide such a description?
DR. ROYER-COLLARD. Oh, no. He's become far too skilled for that. He leaves us hanging with a few vague phrases. We're forced to supply *our own* salacious detail!
COULMIER. But that's preposterous! This tale is nothing but a sentimental romance, as toothless as it is predictable.
DR. ROYER-COLLARD. Don't be so *naive*, Abbe! The story ripples with innuendo! Note Marie's fickle nature. She can't choose a single fabric, no. She begs to try them all! A sly allusion to her promiscuity. She is clearly a nymphomaniac, as inconstant in her taste in men as she is in clothing.
COULMIER. She is?
DR. ROYER-COLLARD. And mark her exorbitance! *Royal velvet!* How, pray tell, will LaFarge afford such luxury? She intends to ruin him! To drive him into crime!
COULMIER. She does?
DR. ROYER-COLLARD. Embezzlement, perhaps, or fraud!
COULMIER. I fear, Doctor, that you've strayed too far from the source —
DR. ROYER-COLLARD. Choose any line of text, and beneath its harmless veneer, you'll find nothing but sin and degeneracy! Go ahead! *I dare you!*
COULMIER. "The Tailor drove the needle through the soft fabric, in and out, in and out, in and out, in and out —"
DR. ROYER-COLLARD. Aha! There! You see!
COULMIER. Good heavens. It's as plain as day, isn't it ...
DR. ROYER-COLLARD. *Copulation!*
COULMIER. One or two well-chosen words, and you can almost see them coupling.
DR. ROYER-COLLARD. Rutting like a pair of dogs! Her robust thighs, parted —

COULMIER.   — her mossy crevice, revealed —
DR. ROYER-COLLARD.   — the battering of his mighty ram —
COULMIER.   — the enveloping lips of her virginal cavity —
DR. ROYER-COLLARD.   — the soft, insistent slapping of skin against skin —
COULMIER.   Her lewd shrieks as he plunges deep into the warm-sepulcher of her woman-flesh!
DR. ROYER-COLLARD.   It's all there, Abbe! Lurking beneath his seemingly flaccid prose!
COULMIER.   Why, the roué! The poltroon!
DR. ROYER-COLLARD.   Exhaustion overtook The Marquis, and so his script tapers. But surely you can divine the story's conclusion!
COULMIER.   I can?
DR. ROYER-COLLARD.   Once wed, the young bride abandons her husband, and decamps with her rapist!
COULMIER.   No! *(Dr. Royer-Collard slams his fists against the desk.)*
DR. ROYER-COLLARD.   THE STRUMPET! THE SCURRIL-OUS LITTLE TRAMP! SHE OUGHT TO BE BOILED! SHE OUGHT TO BE HOISTED ON A PIKE!
COULMIER.   Surely we could posit other outcomes ...
DR. ROYER-COLLARD.   In the world of The Marquis, what other possibilities exist? *Only catastrophe. (He sinks into his chair, his chest concave.)* Poor, gullible LaFarge. He offered everything to the duplicitous little snit. His unwavering devotion. High social station. An opulent home, no doubt, with Italian tile, and a garden full of imported tulips ... *(Tentatively, Coulmier reaches to touch Dr. Royer-Collard's shoulder, to comfort him.)*
COULMIER.   Shhh ... Doctor ...
DR. ROYER-COLLARD.   And what did she proffer instead? Nothing but heartbreak. Now LaFarge is left alone. His love, lost. His reputation, past repair. His very post in jeopardy.
COULMIER.   I can't help noticing that this particular tale has affected you more than the rest.
DR. ROYER-COLLARD.   Though I'm loathe to admit it, as a result of his persistence, his writing has improved. It now boasts a certain ... prescience ... it didn't have before. *(He*

sighs a final sigh, then regains his severe demeanor.) You may pack your bags, Abbe. A carriage awaits, ready to transport you a great distance from Saint-Maurice.

COULMIER.   What's this?

DR. ROYER-COLLARD.   I've arranged for your re-assignment to a monastery in Avignon. There, rather than tending the infirm, you'll transcribe huge, Latin tomes by candlelight.

COULMIER.   With no warning, Doctor? No chance for reprieve?

DR. ROYER-COLLARD.   I am tendering my resignation to the Ministry, effective immediately.

COULMIER.   You too, Doctor?

DR. ROYER-COLLARD.   It's *pre-emptive*, Abbe. I was entrusted to forge order from chaos; and what has transpired since my arrival here? Murder and mayhem — events which, regrettably, do little to enhance my curriculum vitae. I prefer to exit with grace, rather than have my job wrested from me in what would undoubtedly prove to be a rather conclusive study in the art of humiliation.

COULMIER.   But what of Charenton?

DR. ROYER-COLLARD.   I am recommending to the Ministry that we close her doors forever.

COULMIER.   But why, I beseech you?

DR. ROYER-COLLARD.   *We don't govern Charenton — he does!* We flatter ourselves his superiors, when — in truth — we dangle from his strings!

COULMIER.   What of the patients? They've no place to go. No manner in which to clothe and nourish themselves.

DR. ROYER-COLLARD.   We'll turn them loose upon the streets. They have learned The Marquis' maxims. Now, let them live by his commandments. Let them kill for their trousers; let them rip bread and meat from the hands of children.

COULMIER.   Don't you see, Doctor? To admit defeat is to endorse his philosophy!

DR. ROYER-COLLARD.   THEN SO BE IT.

COULMIER.   I CANNOT AND WILL NOT ACCEPT THESE TERMS. *He has yet to conquer me!*

DR. ROYER-COLLARD. *That's enough, Abbe!* Now go. Before the coachman leaves without you.

COULMIER. The principles we espouse here, the ideals we embrace, are the very rudiments of Christian thought! They have weathered the centuries, and cast the world in its present shape! And The Marquis.... Ha! He's nothing but a pustule on the face of history! Stand him on a pedestal next to Christ, and you will see — *he is a puny creature! (He falls to his knees before Dr. Royer-Collard.)* I implore you, sir, give me one more chance. I must see him quelled. Otherwise, I shall never again have the courage to face the glass. *(A long pause, and then:)*

DR. ROYER-COLLARD. Very well. Since you insist ... *(Coulmier kneels before Dr. Royer-Collard.)*

COULMIER. I offer all my gratitude, and place my reputation at your feet.

DR. ROYER-COLLARD. Hold fast to your noble purpose. To revenge the death of a helpless child. To preserve the sanctity of Charenton.

COULMIER. To keep our gates open, and our chambers full.

DR. ROYER-COLLARD. Go then, and do as your heart commands you!

Scene 6

Coulmier, The Marquis.

COULMIER. A VERBOSE INSULT, MARQUIS! *(He gestures to the words which cover The Marquis' room.)* The snide carping of a jaded bombast! A cruel satire of conventional mores! AND MASKED AS A HARMLESS LOVE STORY! This time, Python, you won't slither past! *(The Marquis, sans tongue, tries to protest.)* THE STORY'S TRUE TONE LIES BETWEEN THE LINES, NOT IN THEM! THAT'S PLAIN TO SEE, MY FRIEND? WHAT TO YOU TAKE ME FOR? A DOLT? I swore I'd confiscate your implements, whatever they might be! Place your hands upon the block. ON THE BLOCK! NOW! Ten venomous quills, each dripping its own poison! *(The Marquis places his hands upon the block.)* What else might you employ as your stylus? Tell me that you'll hold a stick in your teeth, and I'll have each molar plucked. Your toes, perhaps, and I'll crack them from the joints. And — yes, oh yes — lest we forget. Your tireless tool, which when engorged, might play the role of plume! That I'll circle 'round a gear, then yank it from its fleshy moorings! WELL, SIR? TELL ME! *(The Marquis, frantic, begins to scribble in the dirt. Coulmier reads:)* "One ... last ... request. A ... dying man's ... plea." *(The Marquis stares at Coulmier, hopefully.)* What is it you want? *(The Marquis goes back to his scratching. Again, Coulmier deciphers the line:)* "Take my manhood last ... so I might savor ... the torture ... till the end ..." *(Coulmier kicks The Marquis in the stomach.)* DOWN, SATAN'S SCRIBE! *(Coulmier yanks The Marquis' head back and intones in his face:)* This time, we'll not waste the surgeon's skills. For such crude cutting, the butcher will suffice! *(A sudden blackout. In the darkness, such sounds! Gears turning. Muscles snapping. The whoosh of a blade through air, and the crunch when it meets its target. The crack of bone, and the popping of joints. The low creak of limbs being stretched. All this, of course, accompanied by appropriate human exclamations. The sounds accumulate, becoming a kind of demented symphony.)*

Scene 7

Dr. Royer-Collard, Coulmier.

Coulmier places a matching pair of tin boxes before Dr. Royer-Collard.

COULMIER.   In this box, you'll find his right hand. In this, his left. No longer will they fashion quills from refuse. *(He places a second set of boxes before Dr. Royer-Collard.)* In this box, you'll find his right foot. In this, its mate. He won't be teaching those nimble toes to write. *(He places a fifth box before Dr. Royer-Collard.)* And last, but not least, the font of his imaginings. In this last box, his tally, whacked.

DR. ROYER-COLLARD.   My, my. You have exceeded my expectations.

COULMIER.   And my own.

DR. ROYER-COLLARD.   And how is the patient faring?

COULMIER.   Poorly. At each extremity, a new wound. To look at him, Doctor, is to see the shape of a man, etched in bandages.

DR. ROYER-COLLARD.   And you? It must've been an ordeal.

COULMIER.   At first, it was unbearable.

DR. ROYER-COLLARD.   And then?

COULMIER.   As you know, the mind serves its owner with surprising elasticity. Though repulsed, I was fueled by the necessity of my actions. And my horror hardened into resolve. Steel purpose. I felt a growing ... interest ... in the proceedings.

DR. ROYER-COLLARD.   Oh?

COULMIER.   I no longer averted my gaze. One box, then two. With austere ceremony, the butcher filled each tiny tomb with tissue and bone. From deep within my core, a quiver. A jolt.

DR. ROYER-COLLARD.   Yes?

COULMIER.   A certain ... satisfaction ... knowing with each chop ... I was taking a step closer to God.

DR. ROYER-COLLARD.   So tell me. Will you sleep soundly tonight?

COULMIER.   No, sir. Plainly put, I never expect to sleep again. *(A brief pause.)* And you?

DR. ROYER-COLLARD.   I worry that our task is not complete.

COULMIER.   I beg your pardon? *(Dr. Royer-Collard taps a finger knowingly on his own forehead.)*

DR. ROYER-COLLARD.   His most potent organ remains intact.

COULMIER.   Please, he's been well-hacked! I left him more meat than man!

DR. ROYER-COLLARD.   Still ...

66

COULMIER.   He flails about on the floor of his cell like some pitiful starfish!

DR. ROYER-COLLARD.   You've broken his body, true. But what about his mind? For all we know, it still composes. What will his next story be, Abbe? Perhaps a tale about a timorous priest ...

COULMIER.   I dare say, Doctor, we can't control his thoughts. We can only mute their expression.

DR. ROYER-COLLARD.   Then we have not truly cured him, have we?

COULMIER.   What murderous act would you have me commit?

DR. ROYER-COLLARD.   Finish the job you've begun.

COULMIER.   These hands cannot ... will not ... extinguish life.

DR. ROYER-COLLARD.   I had hoped they were the hands of a hero.

COULMIER.   You've hands of your own. Why not use them? Why let a minion perform the deed, and usurp the glory? *Or do you, too, fear the stains?*

DR. ROYER-COLLARD.   You've done the worst. The rest is mere formality.

COULMIER.   Good-bye, Doctor. I'll spend one final night in my quarters here, and tomorrow set out for regions beyond.

DR. ROYER-COLLARD.   He lies there, hobbled, fermenting in his own filth. One breath away from salvation. It's in your power to deliver him safely there.

COULMIER.   I've given my answer; it won't change.

DR. ROYER-COLLARD.   Abandon Charenton, and you abandon God.

COULMIER.   I pray that Fate never again ushers me through these portals, or casts my shadow against your door.

Scene 8

Coulmier, The Ghost of Madeleine.

The charnel house.

Coulmier kneels before the casket containing the body of Madeleine.

COULMIER.   Before I take my leave, a final tarry here. To beg forgiveness, dear Madeleine, for your unkind end. Dear God, pity me! Hold her fast by Your side, so that — in heaven — we might be reunited. There I shall fall to my knees, and beg her mercy evermore. *(He leans over to kiss the coffin. It opens. Madeleine bolts upright. Her body has been restored; there's no trace of the horror which befell her at the end of the first act. Her body is bathed in a celestial glow. The trills of an angelic chorus waft through the air.)*

MADELEINE.   Oh, Abbe! Freed at last from this pine box! Unearthed by your pleas!

COULMIER.   What's this? Sweet Madeleine's specter? *(He falls to his knees. He takes Madeleine's hand, and presses her palm to his cheek.)* You're an angel, aren't you, sent to deliver me? I've committed such inhuman, such appalling acts ... tell me I've still some small hope of redemption.

MADELEINE.   When I was stabbed through and through by the madman Bouchon, I fell into the very darkest slumber. When I awoke, I was nestled in the bosom of Our Lord Jesus Christ. It was as if the very earth had risen in the shape of a man, and gathered me in its tender embrace. *(The walls split, and a resplendent Figure of Christ appears, portrayed by none other than The Marquis.)* "Savior," I whispered, too awed to speak any louder, "If only you would kiss my wounds, and make them heal." And so He did. When His lips met the gash on my cheek, the flesh closed, new and rosy. When He pecked the bruise on my knee, it was gone. Soon, my body was again pristine, each mark of the lunatic's blade, abolished. But alas, sir.

Christ's potent kisses did not cease. His mouth no longer sought my lesions; it went after sweeter fruit.

COULMIER.   What impiety is this?

MADELEINE.   "Oh, Holy One," cried I, crossing my legs to thwart his advance, *"I am not injured there."*

THE MARQUIS.   "You've so often worshipped at my temple —"

MADELEINE.   — was his reply —

THE MARQUIS.   "That now I long to worship yours."

COULMIER.   Mademoiselle, if you wish to be spared the tortures of hell, then cease this abomination!

MADELEINE.   I merely report these events! I am not their agent! And then — oh, Abbe! It was then I saw the mask slip from its perch upon his nose. This was no Son of God, but His Inverse. *(The Figure of Christ swivels his mask; now he is Satan.)*

THE MARQUIS.   THERE IS NO GOD BUT ME!

MADELEINE.   *And then, Satan parted his vestments, to reveal his carnal staff.*

COULMIER.   I'll have no more of this ghastly tale!

MADELEINE.   How it defied biology! Less like the fountain of man, and more fitting to a sea serpent! Such tentacles! Yes, 'tis true! His wand was *triple pronged!*

THE MARQUIS.   The Father, the Son, and the Holy Ghost!

MADELEINE.   With that blood-engorged Trinity, he plumbed my throat, my matrix, and that narrowest of strictures which Nature most conceals! My every breach was corked! The Devil's hot rain shot through me like quicksilver!

THE MARQUIS.   IN NOMINE PATRIS ET FILII ET SPIRITU SANTU. AMEN. *(The walls close on the Figure of Satan. Madeleine's voice is now the voice of a skilled seductress.)*

MADELEINE.   *When my legs were opened, so were my eyes. Ooh, Abbe! Now in Death I can freely taste what in Life modesty so cruelly forbade.*

COULMIER.   You are not Madeleine! You're nothing but a succubus, disguised! *(During the following passages, Madeleine strokes Coulmier gently, her hands wandering across his body like moths along a wall. In spite of his best efforts to the contrary,*

69

Coulmier is steadily aroused.)
MADELEINE.   *How you sucked me from death with a single kiss
on the lid of my coffin. What other tricks does that sweet mouth know?*
COULMIER.   Unhand me, I beg you ...
MADELEINE.   *Don't you like my touch?*
COULMIER.   There are vows, more potent than man's pri-
mal stirrings ...
MADELEINE.   *Vows? To whom?*
COULMIER.   To God.
MADELEINE.   *What God?*
COULMIER.   The one you have so clearly forsaken.
MADELEINE.   *Oh, Abbe. What a solid ridge of bone. I'll draw it
slowly into my own thin fissure. There, in a velvet vice, I'll milk it
dry.*
COULMIER.   I beseech you, not there ... *(He is enflamed.)*
MADELEINE.   *Tell me, beloved. Who needs your God now? (She
seizes Coulmier and kisses him. He breaks away urgently; his resis-
tance is spent.)*
COULMIER.   All right then, witch. I'll speak to you in the
only language that you know. I'll drive my own stake through
your wretched center, and pin you forever in the grave. *(He
thrusts Madeleine into the coffin, and climbs atop her. Suddenly, in
his arms, she goes limp. Her body is still, and breathless.)* What's
this? All breath left her body? Oh, God. Her limbs ... the
stench of her flesh ... *(He shrinks back from the casket, horrified.)*
SPIRIT! ANSWER ME! DID THE MARQUIS BID YOU TO
VISIT ME, OR DID YOU BURST — UNCHECKED — FROM
MY OWN BRAIN? TELL ME, I BEG YOU! HAS HE SO LONG
POLLUTED ME, THAT MY OWN DEMONS ARE NOW DIS-
LODGED? *(Coulmier slams the lid of the coffin shut with urgent
resolve.)* I am a priest. I don't have the capacity for such heresy.
*(Coulmier beats both fists on the lid of the casket. He looks heaven-
ward, and asks with murderous intensity:)* WHOSE FANTASY WAS
THIS? WHOSE?

Scene 9

Coulmier, The Marquis.

By now, of course, The Marquis is in a state of hideous disrepair. Coulmier prays, quietly.

COULMIER. Dear Heavenly Father. I could not render this last act if it weren't for the knowledge that I'll be setting this pagan free. That he will be liberated from a society he deems monstrous in design; and that, in turn, all France shall be free from his perdition. And so — with a single, tiny blow — let a greater good flourish from this grisly command. *(Coulmier stands. He turns gently to The Marquis.)* Your head — my poor, misguided man — upon the block. *(Blackout. A loud thwarp, followed by a wrenching tear. Next, a long roll, like a heavy ball cascading down an incline. Finally, a dull thud.)*

Scene 10

Renée Pélagie, Dr. Royer-Collard.

Newly atop Dr. Royer-Collard's desk, a tin box large enough to contain a human head. It rests heavily in the room, like an evil portent. Dr. Royer-Collard sits behind it.

Renée Pélagie enters, in resplendent dress.

RENÉE PÉLAGIE. Good heavens, Doctor! Swing open the shutters! Never did heaven proffer a more beauteous morn!
DR. ROYER-COLLARD. Darkness befits the day's solemnity, Madame.
RENÉE PÉLAGIE. I haven't much time. Madame Miramond had me to breakfast in her garden this morning — oh, such a meal! Plum rosettes floating in cognac, profiteroles bursting

with cream, braised ham shank, steamed rhododendrons — it's all I can do to stand! And tonight — *Mon Dieu!* — it's off to Paris! To the opera! *An opening!* Commissioned by none other than Empress Josephine! My confidante and occasional paramour — the dear Monsieur Baudoin — has given me a ruby tiara to commemorate the occasion! *(She dissolves into giggles of delight.)* Yes, it's me! It's truly me! Renée Pélagie Cordier de Montreuil! *The toast of France!*

DR. ROYER-COLLARD.   Your social schedule has markedly improved.

RENÉE PÉLAGIE.   Indeed it has! My days have become one endless fete, each dancing into the next without pause. And I have you to thank for it!

DR. ROYER-COLLARD.   Is it because we have — once and for all — silenced your husband's muse?

RENÉE PÉLAGIE.   On the contrary. It's because he has received such atrocious treatment at your hands.

DR. ROYER-COLLARD.   What's this?

RENÉE PÉLAGIE.   He's turned from monster to martyr overnight. There are those who swear that your actions against my husband exceeded his prose.

DR. ROYER-COLLARD.   I don't believe it!

RENÉE PÉLAGIE.   You know how people gossip. "Did you hear? They bled The Marquis with a hundred leeches!" Or better still, "They broke his fingers, so he couldn't hold his quill!" Why, it smacks of the Terror! The story currently in circulation ... *l' histoire du moment* ... it's too absurd, really, you'll think me daft ... is that The Marquis — once an able bodied man — *has been disassembled!* Don't blanch, Doctor! It's ludicrous, I know! They say he lies in seven separate — *(She takes note of the boxes strewning the desk. She counts them. She gasps, then turns white.)* Oh, Good God! *(Dr. Royer-Collard begins to fervently argue in his own defense:)*

DR. ROYER-COLLARD.   Recall your desperation! The poignancy of your call to see him stifled! We did your bidding, nothing more.

RENÉE PÉLAGIE.   *My* bidding, sir? I bade you kill the author — not the man!

DR. ROYER-COLLARD.   If our measures seem extreme ...
unorthodox ... *well, so was the patient.*
RENÉE PÉLAGIE.   Yes. Indeed. That he was ...
DR. ROYER-COLLARD.   I pray that you see the necessity of
our action here. And that you will one day — when your grief
abates — commend the wisdom which prescribed so conclusive a remedy. *(Renée Pélagie gingerly advances toward the desk.*
Mustering her courage, she gazes at each box, one by one. When she
reaches the box containing the Marquis' head, she stops.)
RENÉE PÉLAGIE.   I don't dare ask. Is this —
DR. ROYER-COLLARD.   It is. *(Renée Pélagie reaches out a quiv-*
ering hand. With sudden resolve, she plants it firmly on the lid of
the box, and lets out a tremulous sigh.)
RENÉE PÉLAGIE.   It's been countless years since I stood in
the same room as my husband. This is not quite the reunion
I had imagined. *(Her eyes well with tears.)* If you please, sir.
Grant a grieving widow a moment alone with the piteous remains of her decimated spouse.
DR. ROYER-COLLARD.   As you wish, Madame. *(He graciously*
steps into the recesses of his office. Renée Pélagie touches her hand to
her lips, then presses a kiss on the top of the box.)
RENÉE PÉLAGIE.   My dear Donatien. If, as penance for the
life you've lived, you now find yourself in the blackest corner of
hell ... be consoled, my darling. *You 're the only man in the world*
who might find heaven there. (She steps away from the Doctor's desk,
and dabs her eyes. Dr. Royer-Collard steps forth from the shadows.)
DR. ROYER-COLLARD.   I must ask you to be plain with me.
Do you intend legal action against the asylum for the loss of
your husband?
RENÉE PÉLAGIE.   Don't be absurd. I owe you lasting appre-
ciation. My star — already on the rise — will soon pierce the
stratosphere! I expect to dine out on his name and your bar-
barity for some time. My only regret is that this turnabout may
cost you dearly.
DR. ROYER-COLLARD.   How so, Madame?
RENÉE PÉLAGIE.   As you can well imagine, people will not
be predisposed to offer their support to a hospital so sorely
besmirched.

DR. ROYER-COLLARD. I hope crass public sentiment won't inhibit your own generosity. After all ... we did put a rather definitive end to your plight.

RENÉE PÉLAGIE. Doctor. Please. Every bank note I tendered would be soaked in my husband's blood.

DR. ROYER-COLLARD. Yes. Of course. Forgive my impertinence.

RENÉE PÉLAGIE. It's one of life's cruel ironies, I suppose, that success for one must always come at the price of another. *C'est la vie! (She heads for the door. She turns.)* Oh, Doctor. Please don't think me forward, but I was aggrieved to hear about your wife. Her rather ... inexplicable ... disappearance. The thought of you, abandoned in that expansive house, shuffling down those endless corridors. Dining solo in that colossal banquet hall. It rattles my heart.

DR. ROYER-COLLARD. Your capacity to empathize, Madame, almost defies plausibility.

RENÉE PÉLAGIE. And now I must be off. I mustn't keep the coachmen waiting. They'll turn randy in the heat, and I'll have no choice but to appease them! *(She turns beet red.)* Oh, dear! How lovely to blush for *pleasurable* reasons! *(She turns wistful.)* Only yesterday I attended a christening. *A christening!* From "Satan's Bride" to "Godmother" in one fell swoop! *(With a flourish, she charges toward her exit.)* Society may be a capricious mistress, but in me she has found a most willing slave! Ta-ta! *(And she is gone. Dr. Royer-Collard sits, ashen.)*

Scene 11

Dr. Royer-Collard, Coulmier.

Coulmier enters.

He carries a small valise, packed with his belongings.

74

COULMIER.   My job is done. I'll be leaving for the coast tomorrow morning.
DR. ROYER-COLLARD.   What's this?
COULMIER.   Charenton is a place for healing. I am no longer fit to walk its halls. In Nature's embrace, I hope to rediscover my true constitution. *(He goes for the door.)*
DR. ROYER-COLLARD.   You can't leave, my friend. *Not now.*
COULMIER.   Why not?
DR. ROYER-COLLARD.   I ... ah ... I have spoken with the Ministry.
COULMIER.   And — ?
DR. ROYER-COLLARD.   They question our course here.
COULMIER.   We accomplished our primary aim. We ceased production of his repulsive prose.
DR. ROYER-COLLARD.   But the cost was somewhat ... in their minds ... drastic. Radicals, ignorant of the facts, have leapt to some rather incriminating conclusions.
COULMIER.   Such as...?
DR. ROYER COLLARD.   That we ... that you ... were less than humane.
COULMIER.   I did nothing without your sanction!
DR. ROYER-COLLARD.   Please, Abbe.
COULMIER.   WHAT?
DR. ROYER-COLLARD.   You know that's not true.
COULMIER.   You incited my every action!
DR. ROYER-COLLARD.   The Marquis incited your actions; not I.
COULMIER.   It was you who cried "He must be silenced, damn the means!"
DR. ROYER-COLLARD.   A night on the rack, yes! Maybe a spin on the wheel! But *vivisection?*
COULMIER.   DID YOUR URGING EVER FALTER?
DR. ROYER-COLLARD.   Circumstances have turned you surly. Interred too long with the beast, you've now become one.
COULMIER.   If I am a vicious cur, then you are surely my Master.
DR. ROYER-COLLARD.   In point of fact, I never touched him.
COULMIER.   I'll speak to the Ministry myself.

DR. ROYER-COLLARD.   The surgeon and the butcher have already testified on my behalf.

COULMIER.   And what did those turncoats spew?

DR. ROYER-COLLARD.   That I never ordained your gruesome measures. And that — during their enactment — I was absent, while you stood by, instructing each dissection. It was even remarked that in one instance — overcome by zest — *you pirated a finger-bone to wear, concealed, 'round your neck.*

COULMIER.   Slander! Perjure! Lies! Let them judge me by my intentions, not the acts themselves. Violence in pursuit of pleasure is one thing. In pursuit of Justice it's another.

DR. ROYER-COLLARD.   And how do you hope to be judged?

COULMIER.   AS ONE WHO DEFENDED THE PUBLIC GOOD!

DR. ROYER-COLLARD.   *The thrill was a mere dividend? (This stops Coulmier, cold.)*

COULMIER.   It's true.

DR. ROYER-COLLARD.   Forgive me.

COULMIER.   When I ordered the surgeon to sever his tongue, I was green, a novice. But when I came for his head, I did so with all the calm malevolence of a Sadean protagonist. Afterwards ... consumed by guilt ... I sought to pay for his flesh with my own. *(He loosens his vestments. His back and chest are a maze of scars, some old, others newly applied.)*

DR. ROYER-COLLARD.   That's enough.

COULMIER.   I took a cane to my back. Soon, my skin toughened, and withstood the lashing. And so I sought the knife. "Surely, " I thought, "If I can weather pain equal to that which I inflicted ... I will be forgiven." But — with each new gash — Christ offered me a sly reward. *Such exquisite stings ...*

DR. ROYER-COLLARD.   Clothe yourself. Now.

COULMIER.   *I can't stop.* My body's become a map of suffering, and I am its obsessed cartographer. I have stared into the face of evil, Doctor. And ... *heaven help me, please* ... I have never seen such terrible beauty. *Who have I become? What am I to do in my defense? (Tenderly, Dr. Royer-Collard restores Coulmier's robe.)*

DR. ROYER-COLLARD.   That will take care of itself in time.

COULMIER. BUT HOW?

DR. ROYER-COLLARD. We intend to publish The Marquis' manuscripts.

COULMIER. *I beg your pardon?*

DR. ROYER-COLLARD. Anonymously, of course. We need not divulge Charenton's name.

COULMIER. *That is the very calamity we sought to prevent!*

DR. ROYER-COLLARD. And now, it is our only recourse.

COULMIER. Recourse against *what?*

DR. ROYER-COLLARD. Against our ruination. Our revenues have dropped precipitously. We have not fed our wards for three days. Even the dogs scavenge. With profits from the sale of his books, we'll establish a trust in perpetuity. Charenton will rise like the proverbial Phoenix. We'll never again be forced to rely on the fickle allegiance of smug, self-righteous philanthropists.

COULMIER. I'll burn them myself, in a pyre, before I let his writing pass from this place. *(Dr. Royer-Collard approaches Coulmier, and takes him gently by the shoulders, sitting him down.)*

DR. ROYER-COLLARD. Think, my boy. The Marquis' own writings are your best rationale. Surely anyone who reads the pollution inscribed therein will thank you for purging its creator.

COULMIER. Why, yes. Yes, of course.

DR. ROYER-COLLARD. A limited edition. The obsessive patients will set the type, and the listless ones can do the binding. Exorbitantly priced, to preclude the riff raff.

COULMIER. No. No, I beseech you. In every home, a copy. Let mothers yank their children 'round, and read his prose with hearty voices. *(He stares, unwavering at Dr. Royer-Collard.)* Let his volume lie by every Bible as its inverse.

DR. ROYER-COLLARD. And why not? Two sides of the same coin. The first book as reviled as the second is sacred. *(Coulmier breaks into a smile. He starts to giggle. His laughter teeters on the brink of desperation.)*

COULMIER. We're left with a riddle, aren't we Doctor?

DR. ROYER-COLLARD. A riddle?

COULMIER. Which book tells the truth about mankind, and

which book lies? (*Dr. Royer-Collard, uncomfortable, shifts his gaze. He picks up the tin box containing The Marquis' head.*)

DR. ROYER-COLLARD.   Might I suggest we make a gift of his skull to the Phrenology Laboratory. They can, I'm certain, divine from its cranial shape those features exclusive to the libertine. What crests of bone distinguish monsters from men. From you, Abbe. Or me.

COULMIER.   Let them conduct their experiments with all due haste. I need ... proof, Doctor ... proof positive for the sake of my soul ... *I am not of his ilk.*

DR. ROYER-COLLARD.   When the lab provides its findings, then I'm certain you shall be released.

COULMIER.   Released? (*A fast blackout, followed by the rumbling echo of a door as it slams ... the turning of a padlock.*)

Scene 12

Coulmier.

Coulmier paces in the cell formerly occupied by The Marquis.

COULMIER.   Valcour! *Pssst, Valcour!* I have such horrendous truths to impart! And no one in the world to tell them to! (*He presses his face against the bars, and whispers urgently.*) At the edge of the earth ... on her last precipice ... where rock cuts into the night sky ... there are no angels to guide us ... no devils to lead us astray. Would that there were! Alas, there's only the lone figure of a man, swirling endlessly in a hollow void! (*He has a sudden thought.*) I beseech you, bring me paper! I'll need reams of parchment, and gallons of ink besides! Valcour! VALCOUR ... (*Lights remain, dimly, on Coulmier in his cell. Meanwhile, in Dr. Royer-Collard's office:*)

Scene 13

The Marquis, Coulmier.

The six tin boxes — containing The Marquis' tongue, his hands, his feet, and his member — still sit upon the desk.

The largest box, containing his head, lies beneath the desk, on the floor.

A tapping sound. It grows more insistent. One of the boxes opens. Tentatively, a severed hand emerges. It explores the desk. Finally, it alights on a second box, and opens it. Out pops its mate.

Together, they twiddle their thumbs.

The box on the floor begins to rattle. It shakes, like a jack-in-the-box about to pop. The clasp jiggles free, and it falls open, revealing the dismembered head of The Marquis.

The head glances up to discover the hands. It speaks:

THE MARQUIS' HEAD.   Ah, my beauties! I knew you'd never desert me! Look. There. On the desk. Sheaths of paper ... an ink-well ... and *a ready quill! (One hand picks up the quill, while the other readies the paper.)* Yes, my children! That's the way! Now listen closely to Papa. We mustn't miss a word. Legibly, please. *(The head of The Marquis begins to dictate; the hands transcribe.)* "Let he who questions the truths I tell pay this final story heed. There was once a virtuous man called the Abbe de Coulmier. It was his life's work to cater to the feeble, with a kind heart and a gentle hand. Sometimes, when the sun struck his hair just so, or he tilted his head at a certain angle, you could almost discern the halo that rested there. Then, one dark day he encountered a rogue. A rogue with a habit, it seems, for writing stories ..." *(The head of The Marquis begins to laugh. The hands twitter, and clap with glee. Alone in his cell, Coulmier crawls to the window and calls again to the guard:)*

COULMIER. A quill, my good man! A QUILL! *A QUILL!* *(The laughter of The Marquis echoes up and down the cavernous chambers of the asylum. The inmates join him. The sound of their cackling causes the walls to shake, and the floor to roll in waves. Blackout.)*

END OF PLAY

PROPERTY LIST

Calling card (RENÉE PÉLAGIE)
2 razors (DR. ROYER-COLLARD)
Purse, with salt (DR. ROYER-COLLARD)
Wooden prod (DR. ROYER-COLLARD)
Small vice grip (DR. ROYER-COLLARD)
Sheath of 1200 papers (DR. ROYER-COLLARD)
Manuscript (THE MARQUIS)
Decanter of wine (THE MARQUIS)
2 wine glasses (THE MARQUIS)
Pieces of torn linen (THE MARQUIS)
Stick (THE MARQUIS)
Carafe of wine (THE MARQUIS)
Shirt with ruffles (MADELEINE)
Snuff box (DR. ROYER-COLLARD)
Note (MONSIEUR PROUIX, DR. ROYER-COLLARD)
Quill (MONSIEUR PROUIX, THE MARQUIS)
Riding crop (MADAME ROYER-COLLARD)
Small tin box (COULMIER)
2 sets of matching tin boxes (COULMIER)
Medium tin box (COULMIER)
Large tin box (COULMIER)
Small valise (COULMIER)
Paper (THE MARQUIS)

SOUND EFFECTS

Crack of thunder
Wind
Gears turning
Muscles snapping
Whoosh of blade through air and the crunch when it
  meets its target
Cracking bone
Popping of joints
Low creak of limbs being stretched
Angelic chorus
A loud "thwarp," followed by a wrenching tear (head
  chopped off), followed by a roll, then a dull thud
Echo of door slamming, then padlocked

NEW PLAYS

• **MERE MORTALS by David Ives, author of *All in the Timing*.** Another critically acclaimed evening of one-act comedies combining wit, satire, hilarity and intellect -- a winning combination. The entire evening of plays can be performed by 3 men and 3 women. ISBN: 0-8222-1632-9

• **BALLAD OF YACHIYO by Philip Kan Gotanda.** A provocative play about innocence, passion and betrayal, set against the backdrop of a Hawaiian sugar plantation in the early 1900s. *"Gotanda's writing is superb ... a great deal of fine craftsmanship on display here, and much to enjoy." --Variety. "...one of the country's most consistently intriguing playwrights..." --San Francisco Examiner. "As he has in past plays, Gotanda defies expectations..." --Oakland Tribune.* [3M, 4W] ISBN: 0-8222-1547-0

• **MINUTES FROM THE BLUE ROUTE by Tom Donaghy.** While packing up a house, a family converges for a weekend of flaring tempers and shattered illusions. *"With MINUTES FROM THE BLUE ROUTE [Donaghy] succeeds not only in telling a story -- a typically American one with wide appeal, about how parents and kids struggle to understand each other and mostly fail -- but in notating it inventively, through wittily elliptical, crisscrossed speeches, and in making it carry a fairly vast amount of serious weight with surprising ease." --Village Voice.* [2M, 2W] ISBN: 0-8222-1608-6

• **SCAPIN by Molière, adapted by Bill Irwin and Mark O'Donnell.** This adaptation of Molière's 325-year-old farce, *Les Fourberies de Scapin*, keeps the play in period while adding a late Twentieth Century spin to the language and action. *"This SCAPIN, [with a] felicitous adaptation by Mark O'Donnell, would probably have gone over big with the same audience who first saw Molière's Fourberies de Scapin...in Paris in 1671." --N.Y. Times. "Commedia dell'arte and vaudeville have at least two things in common: baggy pants and Bill Irwin. All make for a natural fit in the celebrated clown's entirely unconventional adaptation." --Variety* [9M, 3W, flexible] ISBN: 0-8222-1603-5

• **THE TURN OF THE SCREW adapted for the stage by Jeffrey Hatcher from the story by Henry James.** The American master's classic tale of possession is given its most interesting "turn" yet: one woman plays the mansion's terrified governess while a single male actor plays everyone else. *"In his thoughtful adaptation of Henry James' spooky tale, Jeffrey Hatcher does away with the supernatural flummery, exchanging the story's balanced ambiguities about the nature of reality for a portrait of psychological vampirism..." --Boston Globe.* [1M, 1W] ISBN: 0-8222-1554-3

• **NEVILLE'S ISLAND by Tim Firth.** A middle management orientation exercise turns into an hilarious disaster when the team gets "shipwrecked" on an uninhabited island. *"NEVILLE'S ISLAND ... is that rare event: a genuinely good new play..., it's a comedic, adult LORD OF THE FLIES..." --The Guardian. "... A non-stop, whitewater deluge of comedy both sophisticated and slapstick.... Firth takes a perfect premise and shoots it to the extreme, flipping his fish out of water, watching them flop around a bit, and then masterminding the inevitable feeding frenzy." --New Mexican.* [4M] ISBN: 0-8222-1581-0

DRAMATISTS PLAY SERVICE, INC.
440 Park Avenue South, New York, NY 10016 212-683-8960 Fax 212-213-1539
postmaster@dramatists.com www.dramatists.com

NEW PLAYS

• **TAKING SIDES by Ronald Harwood.** Based on the true story of one of the world's greatest conductors whose wartime decision to remain in Germany brought him under the scrutiny of a U.S. Army determined to prove him a Nazi. *"A brave, wise and deeply moving play delineating the confrontation between culture, and power, between art and politics, between irresponsible freedom and responsible compromise."* --London Sunday Times. [4M, 3W] ISBN: 0-8222-1566-7

• **MISSING/KISSING by John Patrick Shanley.** Two biting short comedies, MISSING MARISA and KISSING CHRISTINE, by one of America's foremost dramatists and the Academy Award winning author of *Moonstruck.* *" ... Shanley has an unusual talent for situations ... and a sure gift for a kind of inner dialogue in which people talk their hearts as well as their minds...."* --N.Y. Post. MISSING MARISA [2M], KISSING CHRISTINE [1M, 2W] ISBN: 0-8222-1590-X

• **THE SISTERS ROSENSWEIG by Wendy Wasserstein, Pulitzer Prize-winning** author of *The Heidi Chronicles.* Winner of the 1993 Outer Critics Circle Award for Best Broadway Play. A captivating portrait of three disparate sisters reuniting after a lengthy separation on the eldest's 50th birthday. *"The laughter is all but continuous."* --New Yorker. *"Funny. Observant. A play with wit as well as acumen.... In dealing with social and cultural paradoxes, Ms. Wasserstein is, as always, the most astute of commentators."* --N.Y. Times. [4M, 4W] ISBN: 0-8222-1348-6

• **MASTER CLASS by Terrence McNally. Winner of the 1996 Tony Award for Best Play.** Only a year after winning the Tony Award for *Love! Valour! Compassion!,* Terrence McNally scores again with the most celebrated play of the year, an unforgettable portrait of Maria Callas, our century's greatest opera diva. *"One of the white-hot moments of contemporary theatre. A total triumph."* --N.Y. Post. *"Blazingly theatrical."* -- USA Today. [3M, 3W] ISBN: 0-8222-1521-7

• **DEALER'S CHOICE by Patrick Marber.** A weekly poker game pits a son addicted to gambling against his own father, who also has a problem but won't admit it. *"... make tracks to DEALER'S CHOICE, Patrick Marber's wonderfully masculine, razor-sharp dissection of poker-as-life.... It's a play that comes out swinging and never lets up -- a witty, wisecracking drama that relentlessly probes the tortured souls of its six very distinctive ... characters. CHOICE is a cutthroat pleasure that you won't want to miss."* --Time Out (New York). [6M] ISBN: 0-8222-1616-7

• **RIFF RAFF by Laurence Fishburne.** RIFF RAFF marks the playwriting debut of one of Hollywood's most exciting and versatile actors. *"Mr. Fishburne is surprisingly and effectively understated, with scalding bubbles of anxiety breaking through the surface of a numbed calm."* --N.Y. Times. *"Fishburne has a talent and a quality...[he] possesses one of the vital requirements of a playwright -- a good ear for the things people say and the way they say them."* --N.Y. Post. [3M] ISBN: 0-8222-1545-4

DRAMATISTS PLAY SERVICE, INC.
440 Park Avenue South, New York, NY 10016 212-683-8960 Fax 212-213-1539
postmaster@dramatists.com www.dramatists.com